PARABLES FROM THE HEART

PARABLES FROM THE HEART

TEACHINGS IN THE TIBETAN ORAL TRADITION

Ringu Tulku Rinpoche

Collated and edited by
Patricia Little, with Mary Heneghan

Bodhicharya
PUBLICATIONS
Awaken the heart by opening the mind

First Published in 2016 by
BODHICHARYA PUBLICATIONS

Bodhicharya CIC, 38 Moreland Avenue, Hereford, HR1 1BN, UK
www.bodhicharya.org   Email: publications@bodhicharya.org

ISBN 978-0-9576398-8-1
First Edition: 2016

Texts selected and collated by Patricia Little. Edited by Patricia Little and Mary Heneghan

Several stories are reprinted here with the kind permission of DHI Publications and Rigul Trust Publications. Titles and full bibliographical references given in 'Sources Used'.

Excerpts from *Path to Buddhahood*, by Ringu Tulku, with the kind permission of NiL Editions (©2003, original French edition ©2001). Excerpts from *Confusion Arises as Wisdom: Gampopa's Heart Advice on the Path of Mahamudra*, by Ringu Tulku, ©2012 Ringu Tulku. And from *Daring Steps Toward Fearlessness: The Three Vehicles of Buddhism*, by Ringu Tulku, ©2005 by Ringu Tulku. Reprinted by arrangement with The Permissions Company, Inc., on behalf of Shambhala Publications Inc., www.shambhala.com. Individual stories credited on the page on which they appear.

Bodhicharya Publications team for this book: Annie Dibble; Conrad Harvey; Mary Heneghan; Patricia Little; Rachel Moffitt; Pat Murphy; Paul O'Connor; Ani Karma Wangmo.

Typesetting & Design by Paul O'Connor at Judo Design, Ireland.
Cover image: Paul O'Connor.
Inside colour image: Chenrezig Thangka painted by Sherab Palden Beru of Kagyu Samye Ling, reproduced with the kind permission of Victoria Long. Photograph by Peter Budd.
Inside line drawings: Conrad Harvey.
Printed on recycled paper by Imprint Digital, Devon, UK.

CONTENTS

Editor's Preface

This collection owes its existence to the perception, shared by many who have been present at Ringu Tulku's teachings, that storytelling is integral to his inimitable teaching style, a dramatic device for awakening or sustaining the interest of his audience, underlining a point, giving tangible form to some aspect of the Dharma to make it memorable. They are an essential part of the oral style, needing an audience to function fully. On the occasion when the story is told, readers who have been present at teachings will recall the way in which Ringu Tulku will court his audience, asking participants: 'Would you like a story now?' and then, with a beaming smile: 'No, you've heard that one before!', which elicits a mock protest from the audience: 'Yes, yes, a story!'

Evoking the living context in which the stories are told, should we therefore conclude that there is a contradiction at the heart of this anthology, that between the oral tradition from which the stories come, and the 'fossilised' form in which they now appear, where the audience has become the reader of a Westernised book? By publishing this sort of material, are we in danger of destroying the very tradition we wish to preserve? The same question can be posed, obviously, with regard to the hundreds of thousands of published Dharma books which we are fortunate enough to be able to buy in any bookshop. We take them home and read them with as much attention as we can muster, finding nourishment in them, but in a sense are we not destroying the tradition in order to preserve it? As Ringu Tulku himself says, 'The Vajrayana is not just about learning and teaching, there is something else, which could be called a heart-to-heart transmission'. It is my belief that the presentation of these parables outside the extended teachings from which they come is a way of preserving this crucial 'heart-to-heart transmission', preventing study of the Dharma from being a merely intellectual affair.

It is largely for this reason that I have presented the stories in three parts: the brief introductory lines in italics represent the context in which the story is to be found, and are usually my summary of what immediately precedes the main body of the text in roman script, the 'Story'. The third part of the presentation, again in italics, summarises the meaning to be drawn from the story, reproducing Ringu Tulku's own words where possible, or, failing that, the spirit of the teaching, with elaboration where necessary. In this way, the vibrant physical and human context in which the story was told is, I hope, recreated. It is perhaps significant, however, that this mode of presentation sometimes comes full-circle, with the 'Teaching' blending seamlessly with the 'Context'.

All the stories selected come from published teachings; where the same story appears in different teachings in slightly modified form, I have indicated this in the footnotes, which are provided only to allow the reader to follow up the particular teaching if (s)he so desires; it is by no means essential. I have adhered in the main to the published form, which generally speaking has preserved the spontaneity of the spoken word, although we have taken the opportunity to make some modifications, including the breaking up of long paragraphs, in the interests of clarity and legibility. Some spellings have also been standardised, for the sake of consistency.

As to the categorisation of the stories, I hesitated whether to group them at all, unwilling to impose a specific interpretation on the reader. In the end, I have tried to group them by theme; but many are so rich in potential sense that they could have been categorised in a very different way. The Jataka tales are a case in point, as are those I have grouped under 'tales of the Great Masters'. In the end, the Dharma is one and indivisible, and this collection is intended to demonstrate that fact.

The essential feature of a 'story' in this context is its narrative character: it evolves in time, representing a sequence of events, and has a particular agent. I have, therefore, excluded what are merely extended images, comparisons, metaphors, which are used to illustrate a point, and which are timeless, however interesting they may be. But these stories are told not just for their entertainment value: they are *parables*, in that they are rich in meaning, and their purpose is to help to lead beings out of samsara.

As to the *dramatis personae*, some real historical characters cross the stage, such as the great founding figures of Tibetan Buddhism – Lord Buddha himself, Milarepa, Naropa, Tilopa, and so forth – but in keeping with their function as vehicles of the Dharma, there is frequently a mythical or hagiographical element to the events depicted. The stories they give rise to are different from those used to illustrate a point of Dharma; I include them in the spirit in which they are told: as an indispensable part of the tradition and as models for samsaric beings. The life of a Lama is in itself a teaching, after all, demonstrating those qualities of perseverance, devotion, and a single-minded search for truth that form the Path out of samsara. These accounts also serve to put in context the hagiographical elements in the presentation of the life of the Buddha.

True to the fundamental tenets of Buddhism, beings are beings, and boundaries between the human and the animal world are frequently crossed as they converse with one another and transform from one realm to another. Ghosts and spirits abound, either benign or malevolent. Animals, especially where they represent a previous incarnation of the Buddha, are conspicuous for their kindness and compassion. The human beings depicted in the folk-tales are prone to the same foibles and weaknesses, their gullibility and their guile, as other samsaric beings, and the fact that they are often not named, being simply depicted generically as 'a man', 'his wife', 'a robber', 'a princess', gives them a universal quality.

I offer these parables to fellow-seekers on the Path in a spirit of true gratitude towards the teacher who, in his wisdom and compassion used them as vehicles for the Dharma, Ringu Tulku Rinpoche.

May all beings have happiness.

Patricia Little
for Bodhicharya Publications

STORIES OF THE BUDDHA, JATAKA TALES

The King, his Queens and the Hermit

(A JATAKA TALE)

Looking at bodhisattva motivation, this teaching reflects on what to do when people are unpleasant or cruel towards us.

One time in a past life, the Buddha was a hermit called Drangsong Zöpa Mawa, who meditated in solitude in a beautiful forest. One day the king came to hunt in this forest, accompanied by his queens and entourage. While the king and his men went hunting, the queens and their attendants stayed behind and wandered into the forest to pick flowers. When the queens came upon the hermit sitting silently in meditation, they were impressed. They made offerings and asked him for teaching, which he granted.

The king returned to find the camp empty and all his queens gone. He had not been fortunate in his hunt, and in a mixture of anxiety and dormant anger he went looking for his queens. He found them sitting around the hermit in what seemed to him to be a somewhat intimate situation. This aroused his anger and he shouted, 'What is this? What are you doing here with all my queens?'

'I am not doing anything,' the hermit replied. 'I am just sitting here, meditating on patience.'

The king, who had a nasty streak, took out his sword and cut off one of the hermit's limbs. He demanded, 'Are you still patient with me?'

The hermit replied, 'Oh yes, I have no hatred for you. You are ignorant and do not know what you are doing'. The king struck him again and it continued in this way. While the king dismembered him, the hermit prayed, 'This king is cutting my body and I feel nothing negative toward him. May I not only forgive him, but once I am enlightened and have gained the necessary wisdom, I pray to be the first person to cut away his ignorance, all his misunderstandings and problems, just as he cuts me now'.

His prayer was so sincere and strong that it came true. When the Buddha reached enlightenment and taught his first five disciples, one of them, Kaundinya, was the first to gain true insight. The Buddha explained that Kaundinya had been this king. Of course, the king had undergone a great deal of suffering for many lifetimes, but eventually the Buddha's compassion led Kaundinya to become enlightened before anyone else.

The most important point for us to learn from this Jataka story is that whenever people react negatively to our good action, we should try to see their situation. Why would they be angry with us? Since people are not angry as long as they are happy, their anger means that they are unhappy and they act negatively because of that. They feel trapped and try to take it out on other people. If we understand their situation, however, we don't need to feel negatively towards them ourselves.

Daring Steps, p. 86-87; variant *Path to Buddhahood*, p. 91.

THE DHARMA REFUGE

The function of the Dharma on the Buddhist path.

There was a man who frequently attended the Buddha's teachings in Banaras over a period of many years.

One day he came to the Buddha and said, 'I have a question for you'.

'Okay', said the Buddha, 'What is your question?'

'Well, I've been coming to your teachings for a long time, and I like what you say very much. But I see that although many people come to your teachings, and one or two really seem to change and attain some tremendous realisation; still it seems to me that many people remain unchanged. Why is that?'

'Where do you come from?' asked the Buddha. 'You don't sound as though you're from Banaras; your dialect is different.'

'I'm from Gaya', the man replied.

'Well,' said the Buddha, 'in that case you must go to Gaya very often'.

'Yes, my family is there; I go back quite often.'

'So you must know the way to Gaya from Banaras very well.'

'Of course. I know the way to Gaya as though it were written on my palm.'

'In that case there must be many people who know that you know the way to Gaya.'

'Oh yes; all my friends know that I know the way to Gaya.'

'So do people come to you to ask for directions to Gaya?'

'Yes; many people come and ask me to tell them how to get to Gaya.'

'Do you tell them?'

'Why not? I tell them every detail. There's no secret about it.'

'And everybody who asks you for the way to Gaya – do they all reach Gaya?'

'No; only those who actually complete the journey arrive there. The rest of them don't.'

'It's the same with me,' said the Buddha. 'I've been to enlightenment, and I know the way. People know I've been there, and they know I know the way, so they ask me how to get there. I tell them all I know; why not? There's no secret; I tell them everything. But only those who actually make the journey arrive there; otherwise they don't.'

It's like that; the Dharma is the way. It's the experience of the Buddha, or of anybody who has explored their way to enlightenment. There is not just one way; there are many ways. Anything that helps us to work on our understanding and to find our true nature is the way. The Dharma is the roadmap, providing the directions. But whether we get to the place it leads to, depends on whether we put it into practice, whether we ourselves walk the path.

Refuge, p.15.

THE FEARLESS PARROT

(A JATAKA TALE)

A teaching on fearlessness.

Once there was a parrot who lived in the forest, and one day the forest caught fire. Since the parrot was able to fly, she started to fly away. Then she heard the crying of the animals and insects trapped in the forest. They could not fly away like she could. When the parrot heard their anguish, she thought to herself, 'I cannot just go away; I must help my friends'.

So the parrot went to the river, where she soaked all her feathers, and then flew back to the forest. She shook her feathers over the forest, but it was very little water, not nearly enough to stop a forest fire. So she went back to the river, wet her feathers, and did this over and over again. The fire was so strong and hot that her feathers were scorched and burned, and she was choking on the smoke. But even though she was about to die, she kept going back and forth.

Up in the god realms, some of the gods were looking down and laughing, saying, 'Look at that silly little parrot. She is trying to put out a forest fire with her tiny wings'.

Indra, the king of the gods, overheard them. He wanted to see for himself, so he transformed himself into a big eagle and flew down just above the parrot. The eagle called out, 'Hey, foolish parrot! What are you doing? You're not doing any good, and you're about to be burned alive. Get away while you can!'

The parrot replied, 'You are such a big bird, why don't you help me to put out the fire? I don't need your advice; I need your help'.

When the little parrot said this with so much courage and conviction, the eagle who, as we have seen, was actually the king of the gods, shed tears because he was so moved. His tears were so powerful that they put out the fire. Some of Indra's tears also fell on the parrot's burned feathers. Wherever the tears fell, the feathers grew back in different colours. This is said to be the origin of parrots' colourful feathers. So it turned out that the little parrot's courage made the fire go out, and at the same time, she became more beautiful than ever.

We need a deep understanding that fear is useless and unnecessary. When something happens to us, we simply have to go through with it. Whether it is good or bad, our only choice is to keep going. Fear doesn't make it any better, although it can make it much worse. We need courage. Without courage, we can become frozen and think, 'I can't do this and I could never do that'. But in fact, you will never get stuck in a situation if you face it with courage.

Confusion Arises, p. 174-5.

　　　　　STORIES OF THE BUDDHA, JATAKA TALES

THE START OF THE BODHISATTVA PATH

The Bodhisattva path.

There is a story in the sutras about how Gautama Buddha first embarked on the Bodhisattva path and first became a Bodhisattva. Buddha told this story himself. He said, 'I generated Bodhicitta when I was born in the hell realm, when I had the horrible experience of being forced to drag a chariot made of solid iron over burning ground along with another person'.

Because the iron chariot was too heavy, there was no way two people could pull it. It was a merciless situation, pitiless and filled with lots of suffering. And Buddha thought to himself, this is a completely impossible situation. How can the two of us pull a chariot that even one hundred people wouldn't be able to pull? It is useless for both of us to suffer. Why not let my companion go?

Turning to the guard he said, 'Please let my friend go away. I will do the work for both of us, alone'. Then it seems that the hellish guard became furious, picked up something heavy and hit him on the head so that he fainted. (They say that to faint in the hell realms is the greatest pleasure.) When he regained consciousness he was no longer in the hell realm, because his intention was too good for that realm to contain. Since he genuinely wished to help his friend and carry the problem alone, he became a Bodhisattva. The Buddha said that was the first time he generated Bodhicitta, and that was when his path to Buddhahood started.

Ideal compassion, ideal Bodhicitta can be described as limitless compassion. But it is also said that it is not necessary to have limitless compassion at the start. You can become a Bodhisattva even if you have very limited compassion.

As told by Ringu Tulku, and communicated by Margaret Richardson. Source unknown.

II

THE PATH OF THE BODHISATTVA

THE MAN WHO VISITED HEAVEN AND HELL

The main practice of relative Bodhicitta.

Perhaps you know the story about the man who visited heaven and hell. First, he went to hell. There was a large table with all the inhabitants of hell sitting around it. The centre of the table was full of delicious food. Each person had two very long chopsticks. They could reach the food but they were unable to get the food into their mouths. The chopsticks were too long, so everyone went hungry.

The man then went to visit heaven. All the inhabitants of heaven were sitting around a big table full of delicious food but they were happy. They also had two long chopsticks, and they were eating and enjoying themselves because they were using the chopsticks to feed each other across the table. The people in heaven had discovered that it was rewarding to subdue their self-interest.

Selflessness brings benefits to the one who exercises it, at the same time allowing the whole community to survive, whereas selfishness leads to its destruction.

Mind Training, p. 34.

The Man with the Big Family

Developing a sense of perspective about our own difficulties develops our compassion for others.

There was once a man who had a big family. He and his wife had many children, and his wife's parents were living with them, and they were all in one small house. It was all very congested and he felt altogether too put upon.

So the man goes to his priest and says, 'Please help me; I'm going mad! There are so many people at home and the children are running about and fighting and my wife and my in-laws are shouting and it's all too much. It's driving me crazy! What can I do?'

And the priest says, 'All right. If you do exactly as I say, you can get out of it'. He says, 'Oh, I'll do anything you say – anything!' So the priest tells him, 'All right. Go and buy a chicken – a live one – and take it home'.

The man goes to the market and buys a live chicken and takes it home. And of course it's even worse. He can't bear it for more than a week. He runs back to the priest and says, 'Now what can I do? It's much worse than before: the chicken is playing with the children and it's making everything dirty and it's all so much worse. What can I do?' 'Oh, don't worry,' says the priest. 'If you do exactly as I say you'll be all right. Now go and buy a goat and take it home with you.'

So he buys a goat and takes it home. And then of course it's completely chaotic, and he can't stand it for even three days before he goes back to the priest, crying, and he sobs, 'I can't bear it any longer. It's completely impossible. Whatever shall I do?' The priest tells him, 'Now you go back and sell the goat'. So he goes back and sells the goat.

And then after one week he comes to the priest and says, 'Oh, I'm so relieved. It's so peaceful now'. And the priest says, 'Now get rid of the chicken too'. So he gets rid of the chicken too (maybe makes nice chicken soup, I don't know!) Then some time later he runs into the priest in the street and says to him, 'Oh, thank you so much for your help. Now everything is quite alright!'

All our problems are relative. Sometimes when people say to me, 'Oh, everything is so bad here; my future is so gloomy,' I suggest, 'Maybe you should go to India and have a look around'. And sometimes they go, and when they come back they say, 'Oh, it's good to be back; it's so nice here!' Just as I don't want to suffer, others don't want to suffer either, and this process of empathy is the main source of compassion.

Buddhist Meditation, p. 26-28; variant Daring Steps, p. 25-26.

THE WOULD-BE BODHISATTVA

The true nature of generosity and compassion.

A man who generated the wish to become a great Bodhisattva made a vow to give people whatever they wanted, and never refuse anybody anything they asked for. So of course everybody came and asked for this and that, and as he was a rich man he could give them whatever they wanted. This went on for quite some time, until one day a particularly difficult customer came along and asked if it was really true that he would give whatever was asked of him.

'That's right. I'm a Bodhisattva. I'm happy to give everyone whatever they want.'

'Then give me your right hand.'

The 'Bodhisattva' didn't hesitate: he asked for a knife and cut off his right hand and gave it. But the man refused to accept it – in fact he was furious! In India the left hand is regarded as unclean. They're very particular about it: you can't even pass the salt or pepper with your left hand – people won't take it.

'You can't give me something with your left hand! That's disgusting!' he shouted.

And according to the story, the would-be Bodhisattva was so shocked and discouraged by this incident that he abandoned his efforts altogether. 'People are impossible to please,' he said. 'That's the end of my Bodhicitta!'

It was a useless thing to do, just giving unintelligently without discriminating between what was and wasn't beneficial; practising compassion should not be like that.

Bodhichitta, p. 8-9; variants *Path to Buddhahood*, p. 79-80, *Daring Steps*, p. 83.

III

LOVE AND COMPASSION

The King, the Hunter and the King of the Deer

(A JATAKA TALE)

The symbolism of the deer-skin worn by Chenrezig.

In this story, a hunter once fell down a cliff and got lost in the jungle. Almost dying, he was crying for help when a beautiful deer appeared and showed him the way out of the forest, thus saving his life. This animal was so extraordinary that the hunter thought the king would reward him for catching it. He told his story to the king and agreed to lead him to the place where he had seen this wonderful animal and help him to catch it, in return for a reward. The king surrounded the forest with his men, who started shooting all the animals they could see.

When the deer heard what was going on, he came face to face with the king and asked him, 'Why are you doing this? You should not kill uselessly and senselessly like this. What do you really want?' Hearing the deer speak, the king was very impressed. He explained that he killed animals because he and his subjects had to eat. The deer replied, 'It is true you have to eat, but you don't need to kill senselessly as you're doing now. I am the king of the deer. If you agree, we can make an arrangement that will be good for all of us. From now on, I will send a deer to your kitchen every day'. Impressed and surprised, the king accepted the deal and returned to his palace.

The next day, a deer appeared at his kitchen door; and the next day, and the next, and every day. But one day, as the king of the deer was walking through the jungle, he heard somebody weeping. Looking around, he saw a doe who was sobbing in despair. When he asked why she was weeping, she answered that it was her turn to go next day to the king's kitchen and that she had just given birth to the small baby lying by her side. Her own death would mean that her baby would surely die too, which was why she was so unhappy. The king of the deer comforted her and told her not to worry, that she wouldn't have to go; the next day, he himself stood near the king's kitchen. He looked so extraordinary that the cooks immediately informed the king that a very special deer had come that day. The king recognised the king of the deer, and asked him:

'Why have you come here yourself? You should have sent one of your subjects.'

'Today I have come myself, so you can kill me and eat me.'

'This is not right! You are such a wonderful being, and you are the king of the deer. I can't kill you. You must go away at once.'

'No, I cannot go because, if I have to send all my people in turn to come to you and be eaten, then when my turn comes, I should also share their fate. If you spare my life because I am the king, how can I deserve my title and lead my people? My turn has come today, so I must take my responsibility.'

The king asked him what he could do to spare his life. The deer answered, 'You can declare that, from now on, you will no longer require any deer to come here to be killed. You can forbid all the people in your country to hunt deer, and not only the deer but all other animals too. All the animals are like us: they are afraid when they are hunted, tortured and killed. If you give this order, then maybe I will go away'.

LOVE AND COMPASSION

The king was so surprised and so moved that he agreed immediately and promised to make this announcement that very day. 'Now you can go away!' he said.

But the deer was still not satisfied. 'The birds in the sky are as badly treated as the other animals by the humans,' he said. 'So are the fishes in the rivers and lakes. How can I be happy if only the forest animals are saved but the birds and fishes are still being hunted? I don't want to leave if I can save only my people, while the other animals are still not free to live their lives happily.'

So the king agreed to issue a royal decree stating that from now on, in his country, nobody would be allowed to hunt or fish or kill any animal, and that every living being would be free. Then the deer thanked the king and went away.

This story shows us the power of giving a noble example: the deer was a truly noble creature, demonstrating selflessness, equanimity and compassion towards other sentient beings. His example inspired the king to give up his senseless hurting of animals and follow more caring action instead. The deer skin Chenrezig wears symbolises this compassion.

Chenrezig, p. 21-23.

The Positive Effects of Meditating on Love and Compassion

The signs and benefits of having developed loving-kindness.

There was once a very powerful evil spirit that visited the camp of a Lama. He walked up and down the camp and no one even saw him. 'All these Lamas are quite useless', he thought. 'I can do any harm I like to any of them.' He went straight to the tent of the highest Lama. He saw a little old person sitting in a meditation box. He went in and sat on the head of this Lama, thinking that he would crush him. But the old Lama did not resist. Instead, he started to become flat, and then he started to laugh. He shrank but never stopped laughing. The evil spirit suddenly became very sad. The more the old Lama laughed, the sadder the spirit felt. He started to cry and could not stop. He cried his heart out and left. For more than a year he was unable to hurt anybody; he couldn't even think about it. The old Lama had been meditating on love and compassion.

Meditating on loving-kindness protects us like armour from all negative influence. Even better, this meditation allows us to help and be helped.

Path to Buddhahood, p. 60.

IV

THE PARAMITAS

THE LAZINESS OF POSTPONING

The Six Paramitas: Diligence.

A Tibetan monk had as a friend a sort of spirit that we call *therang* in Tibetan. These dark and very hairy goblins have only one foot and love to play dice. It is said that, in order to make friends with one of them, one should go to a place where three rivers converge, throw dice, and repeat, 'I win; the therang loses!' until the temptation gets too strong for the therang, who holds out his big hairy hand and says, 'No! I'm not losing! Give me the dice!' One must then grab his hand and say, 'I won't let you go unless you become my friend!'

Thus a therang and this monk had become friends. They lived together in the monastery, the therang bringing the monk everything he wanted. The monk lived very happily in luxury. Although he knew very well that he should practise, he would postpone it all the time. He told his friend, 'Certainly I am very happy right now, but I must practise to prepare for death. Warn me as soon as you see my death approaching'. The therang agreed.

Months and years passed until one day the therang said to his friend, 'Lama, do you realise your hair has gone grey?' The monk replied, 'Of course my hair is grey. I'm getting old!' The therang went off, thinking, 'Everything is okay, he knows'. A few years later, the therang told him, 'Lama, you're losing your teeth'. The monk replied, 'Of course I'm losing my teeth. I am getting old!' The therang thought, 'If he knows this, all is well'.

One day, the therang announced to his friend that he was going to die on the following day. The monk got angry and reproached his friend: 'Why didn't you tell me earlier? I asked you to warn me!' The therang replied, 'But I warned you loads of times. First I told you your hair was going grey – you told me you were getting old, so I thought you realised. Then I told you your teeth were falling out, and again you told me you knew. I warned you many times!' This time the monk was seriously anxious, but what could he do now with so little time left?

This type of laziness is treacherous because illusions delude us into a sense of security. We truly believe we're going to do everything we should, but, for one reason or another, we're always putting things off until later. In order to avoid falling into this trap, we must stimulate our diligence.

Path to Buddhahood, p. 94-95.

Anathapindada Learns Generosity

The Six Paramitas: Generosity 1

One of the Buddha's disciples, later known as Anathapindada, was a rich businessman who attended the Buddha's teachings with great enthusiasm. But whenever the Buddha spoke of generosity, Anathapindada found himself unable to relate to it. One day he addressed the Buddha and said, 'I like your teachings very much, but whenever it comes to generosity, I find it totally beyond me. I cannot give anything away. Even the thought of it is painful'.

The Buddha replied, 'If you practise, you might become more generous'. Anathapindada said, 'How can I practise? It is impossible for me to give anything'. The Buddha asked him, 'Can you give something to yourself?' When Anathapindada said he could, the Buddha said, 'Take something in your right hand and give it to your left hand. Then, have your left hand give it back to your right hand. Keep doing this and it may make you more generous'.

Anathapindada followed his advice; he went home and took a piece of gold and gave it to his left hand and said, 'Take it!' Then he gave it to his right hand and said, 'Take it!' In this way, he slowly became more generous, until finally he was one of the greatest benefactors of his time, setting up houses throughout the country to feed and shelter the poor. He thus earned the name 'Anathapindada', which means 'one who is generous and altruistic'.

This shows that generosity is not just a matter of giving. It means being rid of our overwhelming attachment to ourselves and whatever we have. That is the main point. Generosity is being spacious and open hearted.

Daring Steps, p. 101; variant *Mind Training*, p. 75-76.

THE OLD LADY WHO
FOUND A GOLD COIN

The Six Paramitas: Generosity 2

It is said that during Buddha's time there was an old lady who found a gold coin. It was a very nice, special gold coin and she thought she wanted to give it to somebody who really needed it. She asked Buddha who was the person who needed it the most. Buddha thought for a while and then he said that if she really wanted to give it to the person who needed it the most, she should give it to this particular man, who was actually the richest person in town.

The old lady was not very convinced but she was very devoted to Buddha so she went to this man and offered him the gold coin. She said, 'I found this gold coin and I asked Buddha who I should give it to and he said you, but I'm not convinced he is right'.

And the man said, 'He is absolutely right! Because I have 999 of the same gold coins and I am desperately looking for one more to make 1,000!'

After 1,000, he will want to make it 10,000. After 10,000, he will want to make it 100,000; then one million. And so on. This attitude of not having enough is not about having or not having. It is a habitual tendency. If you are not satisfied, you can have the whole world and still not be satisfied.

Journey from Head to Heart, p. 79.

The Big Fish and the Small Fish

The Six Paramitas: Wisdom.

I once saw a cartoon in a Chinese magazine on Zen. It showed a big fish and a small fish in the middle of the ocean. The small fish asked, 'Where is the sea? Everybody keeps talking about the sea, but I don't see it. Where is it?' The big fish said, 'Oh it's all around you'. The small fish was bewildered and said, 'But what is all around me?' The big fish replied, 'You are in it. All around you, up and down, everywhere is the sea'. The small fish said, 'Well, what is it? I don't see any sea around me!'

When we practise the Paramita of wisdom, we are not trying to see something that is totally different or completely beyond us. We are trying to attain the wisdom of seeing ourselves and everything around us clearly, as it truly is.

Daring Steps, p. 107.

V

WISDOM VERSUS LEARNING

TRUTH AND DOGMA

A teaching on the limitations of intellectual understanding in the context of meditation.

There is a story from the Christian tradition that I like very much. One day the devil was sitting on a cloud surrounded by his retinue. Looking down on the earth they saw a man walking back and forth, again and again, intensely searching for something. Suddenly a brilliant light surrounded him, so clear and magnificent a light that he had obviously discovered something truly significant. 'What happened?' the devil's followers asked. 'He found the truth', the devil replied. Hearing that, they became very nervous and said, 'He found the truth? This is terrible; it will be the end of us. Aren't you worried?' The devil said he wasn't, and when they asked him why, he said, 'So, he found the truth. But as soon as he talks to someone else, they will turn it into a dogma. Why should I worry? There's no problem at all'.

As far as truth is concerned, in meditation as in anything else, we have to find it ourselves through direct experience. What we usually relate to is the image of truth we have created in our mind. This image is not enough. We need to arrive at the direct and immediate vision of the truth, which is uncontrived and free from any artificial additions.

Daring Steps, p. 199-200.

THE LIMITS OF LEARNING

Just studying everything from beginning to end, and just intellectually knowing everything about the whole Buddhist Canon, the whole Buddhist philosophy, does not really mean too much. You can recite the whole Kangyur and Tengyur, but of what help will it be? This is illustrated by a story from the Buddha's life.

One of the Buddha's assistants had been serving him for a long time, and he had heard a lot of teachings, which he knew by heart and was very proud. Once he got a little annoyed, and he left the Buddha. Wherever he went, he used to tell people, 'Except for a kind of radiance emanating from his face and body, the Buddha is not different from me. I know whatever he knows'.

He actually knew all the teachings by heart, but it did not help him. It did not benefit him because he had not practised anything and his life did not end very nicely.

Ngöndro, p. 11.

VI

MINDFULNESS
AND RIGHT
UNDERSTANDING

THE MAN WHO HAD VISIONS IN RETREAT

The difficulty of assessing the quality of visions.

I heard about a man in a three-year retreat in Canada who heard a voice saying to him, 'You should go out and do something to benefit beings. You are wasting your time here, just doing retreat'. This happened over and over.

The man thought this was a good idea, so he left retreat. He went to see a Lama – I think it was Kalu Rinpoche – and told the Lama about this sign that he needed to go out and work for the welfare of others. The Lama told him, 'No, that was an obstacle for your retreat. You should immediately go back in'.

But the student did not go back. He left, and as he tried to work for others, everything went wrong. He couldn't accomplish anything, and then he started drinking and became an alcoholic. He was kicked out of the place where he was living and had to live on the streets. After several years, he realised he had been mistaken. So he went back into retreat, and after completing a three-year retreat, he eventually went into lifelong retreat.

A good vision makes you feel very positive and warm-hearted, makes you more compassionate. Negative visions make you uncomfortable, dissatisfied, or depressed.

Confusion Arises, p. 113-14.

THE WISE SHEPHERD

The way in which our mind determines our experience.

There was once a wise shepherd who used to graze his sheep near a mountain pass above his native village. One day a stranger came by and enquired, 'What kind of people live down in that village?'

The shepherd asked in return, 'What kind of people live in the village you came from?'

'Oh, they are horrible', the stranger replied. 'They are nasty and inhospitable.'

The shepherd said, 'Well, the people down there are just the same. They are quarrelsome and totally lacking in hospitality'. Hearing that, the stranger turned back and went somewhere else.

Some time later another traveller arrived and asked the same question. Again the shepherd enquired, 'What kind of people live in the village you came from?'

'Oh, they are wonderful,' the second stranger replied. 'They are warm-hearted and friendly.'

To him the shepherd said, 'Well, you will find the people down there are just the same. They are very good and hospitable to everyone'. So the traveller continued on to the village.

The way we experience our environment depends on our reactions and habits. Since wherever we go we take ourselves with us, we will meet, more or less, the same kind of people everywhere. Therefore we should do our best to tame our own mind.

Daring Steps, p. 94; variant Ngöndro, p. 25.

RINGU TULKU'S STUDY OF MATHEMATICS

Reflections on learning the basics.

When I was young I wanted to make cars and aeroplanes and people told me that I needed to study mathematics first to learn this. So I bought some small books on geometry and algebra and went to a friend who had been to school, to learn from him. When we opened the geometry book, there was a diagram, a triangle with the letters *a*, *b* and *c* at each corner.

'What are these a, b, c?' I asked.

'Well, they are imaginary points', he answered.

'What is an imaginary point?'

'Well, you just have these points, and you call them a, b, and c.'

'What does "a" mean?'

'Nothing, it's just an imaginary point.'

'And "b"?'

'Well, just another imaginary point.'

'How can "a" mean nothing, and "b" nothing either? It must mean something, why then "a"?'

'No, no, it is not necessarily "a", it could be d, e, f, or z, anything!'

It was completely beyond my understanding, so that was my last class on geometry! I then thought that mathematics was very difficult. Much later, as a grown-up, I taught at the university and there was a mathematics department. I told the professor that I thought mathematics was completely beyond my scope of understanding and he asked me why. I told him the story and explained my problem. Then he said, 'No, it is easy. Suppose you are building a house from here to there, the distance is this much, the width and height are that much. Then you make a point here, and there, and you measure it. And then you know how many bricks you need'. So it became very clear. If my first teacher had explained it like that from the beginning, maybe I would now be a mathematician! I think it is like that with everything. If you miss the basics, then you will not know what you're talking about.

This is true also for Dharma practice. Sometimes you do things, but you don't know what you're actually doing. When you recite something every day, it seems to be all right, but when you really want to know what each word means, it is sometimes quite difficult. However, if you don't understand the basics of the practice properly, you don't understand anything. Therefore, it is very important to try to understand the elementary things one by one, both through analysis and from an experiential point of view. We must have a thorough grasp of the Preliminary Practices before embarking on the study of high Mahamudra.

Ngöndro, p. 2-3.

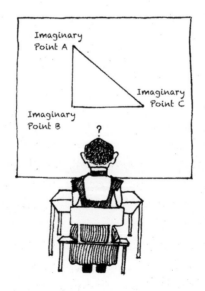

MINDFULNESS AND RIGHT UNDERSTANDING

THE BRAHMIN AND HIS GOAT

A warning to investigate our own deluded motives and not to rely on the opinions of others.

Once a Brahmin was taking his goat to a nearby town. Four young men of doubtful character saw him coming and decided to trick him out of his goat. After they had laid their plot, one of the young men approached the Brahmin and said, 'What a nice dog'. For Brahmins dogs are impure animals, so it is not surprising that he was outraged.

'This is not a dog; it's a goat!' he exclaimed.

'Well', the young man said, 'it looks like a dog to me'. Then he continued on his way.

After some time another of the young men walked towards the Brahmin and asked him, 'Where are you going?'

'I am going to town', he answered.

'Why are you taking that dog with you?' the young man enquired.

The Brahmin said, 'I am not taking a dog; I am taking my goat'.

'That isn't a goat,' the young man insisted, 'that is a dog. You are taking a dog'.

The Brahmin was bewildered by now and shouted, 'No, you must be crazy!' The young man gave in and went away.

Then the third man passed by and the Brahmin asked, 'Am I taking a goat with me?'

'No, you are taking a dog', the man replied. By now the Brahmin was beginning to panic and hurried on.

When the fourth man came his way, he said, 'Come here! What is this? Do you see a dog or a goat?'

The young man shook his head, 'Of course, I see a dog'. At that the Brahmin left the goat on the spot and ran away. So, the four men got his goat as they had planned.

This shows how misleading it can be when we rely too much on the opinions and statements of other people, mistrusting our own innate wisdom.

Daring Steps, p. 109.

THE SHEPHERD AND THE TWO BAGS OF PEBBLES

A teaching on awareness and training in mindfulness.

Once there was a shepherd who was tending his herd in the mountains. A renowned Lama lived in a cave nearby. The shepherd had heard many things about him, that he was a highly realised Lama. Students came from faraway places to see him. One day the shepherd visited the Lama and said, 'I am a simple shepherd. I know nothing. I am illiterate, but I want to do some Dharma practice. Would you give me a practice that requires no understanding, knowledge or education, just a simple practice a most ignorant person could do?'

The Lama responded, 'Take two small bags and fill one with white pebbles and the other with black pebbles. When you sit on a rock while watching over the sheep, keep the two bags near you and just look at yourself, watch your mind. If a negative emotion arises in your mind, take a black pebble and place it on your left side. If a good emotion arises in your mind, then place a white pebble at your right side. Just do that and nothing else'.

The shepherd did as the Lama suggested. He filled his two bags with black and white pebbles and watched his mind. During his practice he noted – one black pebble, two black pebbles, ten black pebbles, fifty black pebbles. No white pebbles! At the end, there were only one or two white pebbles. So he was very worried and concluded, 'This is not good. This is a very bad practice'.

He returned to the Lama and complained, 'This is not good. The black pebbles are growing into a mountain and there are only two or three white pebbles'.

The Lama answered, 'It doesn't matter. Just keep on doing that. Place the pebbles in the bags and start anew every day'.

The shepherd did as he was told, again and again. Slowly, slowly, after several months, the white pile grew and the black pile became smaller.

Whatever we are doing in our daily lives, we should be aware of the state of our mind. When we notice our mind is positive and peaceful, it's like placing a white pebble on the pile. When our mind is negative, and we become aware of it, it's like placing a pebble on the black pile.

Dealing with Emotions, p. 55-56; variants *Ngöndro*, p. 34, *Daring Steps*, p. 41.

MINDFULNESS AND RIGHT UNDERSTANDING

VII

THE SPIRITUAL FRIEND

COMMUNICATING PROPERLY WITH STUDENTS

One of the qualities of ordinary spiritual friends.

A monastery in Gangtok had many monks, mainly Bhutanese. The abbot invited a *khenpo* [great scholar] who was a native of the Tibetan province of Kham to teach the monks. For two years he taught every morning and evening. It was only at the end of the second year that he realised that his students spoke a different dialect and had understood absolutely nothing of his teachings. Deeply disappointed, he dropped everything and returned to Tibet. He was an excellent teacher, but because he could not communicate with his students, he couldn't help them.

Keep your eye on the basics!

Path to Buddhahood, p. 26-27.

The Choice of a Master

The importance of choosing one's master well, but also of not putting this choice off for too long.

Long ago, a Chinese emperor invited Sakya Pandita, a great Tibetan Lama, to his court. When Sakya Pandita arrived, the emperor announced that he had to examine whether he was worthy of becoming his master. He examined him for three years and finally declared that he accepted him as his master. Sakya Pandita replied that he, in turn, had to decide whether he could accept the emperor as a disciple. He died before giving his answer.

The master-disciple relationship is reciprocal.

Path to Buddhahood, p. 30.

VIII

DEVOTION

The Lama and the Yogi

A teaching on devotion and its transformative power.

There is a story about a Lama and a famous yogi who both lived in Kham, eastern Tibet. The Lama eventually reached a high level of attainment and later in his life became very renowned. When he was young, however, he was somewhat taken in by the strong experiences that arose from his practice, and at that time he thought that he must have attained real accomplishment.

The yogi, in contrast, was a truly great master. He stayed in a cave in the mountains and never kept any belongings whatsoever. Whenever he was offered a gift, he immediately let it roll down the slope beneath his cave to be picked up by the beggars who knew of his ways. He hardly ever spoke; he just sat in his cave, and whoever approached him would receive his blessing and then go away.

One day the Lama decided to see this yogi and thought to himself, 'Today I will show him how good I am!' He sat down in front of the yogi and immersed himself in the deepest meditation he could perform. After some time he looked up, but the yogi did not seem to be pleased. He was obviously not impressed at all. Realising this, the Lama felt slightly hurt that his outstanding capacities were not appreciated. In his grief he remembered his guru and spontaneous devotion arose in him. Then, he became totally immersed in his devotion and sat there for quite a while, not doing anything.

When the Lama became conscious of the world again, the yogi was very pleased and showed him by a sign that this time he had done very well. He had been in real meditation whereas before he was just displaying his pride.

This story shows the significance and value of devotion.

Daring Steps, p. 196-197.

The Story of the Dog's Tooth

A teaching on the nature of devotion and the way in which it goes beyond the object that inspires it.

There was once a Tibetan merchant who travelled regularly to India for his business. His mother was very pious. The first time he left for India, she asked him to bring back some relics from the Buddha, as he was going to this very holy country, the very place where the Buddha had lived and taught. But the son forgot. The next time, his mother repeated her request, but the son forgot again. This happened several times. Then the mother threatened her son, 'I am getting old and I may die soon. Now, this time, if you don't bring me back some relic from the Buddha, I will kill myself in front of you!' But once again, the son forgot.

However, on his way back, he remembered his mother's words. Tibetans are very stubborn, and he knew that his mother was perfectly capable of doing what she had threatened and killing herself in front of him. He was not very far from his village so, in desperation, he looked around where he was, to see if there was anything he could bring to his mother. Then he saw the skeleton of a dog. He took off one of its teeth, cleaned it, polished it a little bit and wrapped it in beautiful Indian silk.

When he arrived home, he gave it to his mother, saying, 'This time, I've brought back your relic, and what a relic! The very tooth of the Buddha himself!' His mother wept with joy and put the dog's tooth on her altar. She would pray and pray all day long in front of it with the deepest devotion. After a while, rainbows and five-coloured rays started shining from the tooth and when the old woman died, many wonderful signs were seen.

The object of our devotion may have its importance, but the emphasis here is on the devotion itself, which transcends in its effect the very ordinary object that inspires it. This is true Guru Yoga.

Like Dreams and Clouds, p. 51.

DEVOTION

THE BANDIT FROM KHAM

Guru Yoga: the more we understand about great masters, the more we will develop devotion, and the better we will understand the practice. This comes about because the more we understand the experiences of the masters who have actually practised and got real experience, the more we understand what the practice is about.

These reflections on devotion remind me of a story. A highwayman, a kind of bandit from Kham, was dying. A Lama came by his side and instructed him to think of the Buddhas, the Lamas and so on. The dying Khampa answered he could not think of them. 'What can you think of?' asked the Lama.

'Well', answered the man, 'all I can think of is this: sausages, sizzling on hot ashes, very hot, bursting a little bit, looking delicious.'

The Lama then told him, 'Actually, the pure land of Dewachen is full of such hot sizzling ash-coloured sausages. They are hanging from every branch of every tree, and you do not even have to pick them up: if you lie down under a tree, they will fall into your open mouth! Even Amitabha Buddha, the main Buddha of this pure land, is also a little bit ash-coloured. Can you now think of that?'

'Oh yes, yes!' answered the highwayman. He then thought of this pure land, felt very inspired, died peacefully and was reborn in Dewachen.

So if all you can think of are sizzling sausages, you can still imagine all the Lamas of the lineage holding sizzling sausages! But maybe you would prefer sizzling potatoes, French fries?! Either way, the point is that your feeling of devotion, overall, is more important than the details.

Ngöndro, p. 97.

THE WISDOM AND COMPASSION OF JESUS

A teaching on devotion, and how it arises.

I can remember being inspired by a Bible story about the wisdom of Jesus Christ. One time Jesus came upon some people throwing stones at a woman in order to kill her. She had misbehaved by being a prostitute or committing adultery or something like that.

Jesus said to the crowd, 'Stop! Wait a minute. You can throw stones at her and even kill her, because she did something wrong. But the first stone must be thrown by someone who has never sinned. Look inside and see if you have ever done something you should not have done. If you have never done anything wrong, then you can pick up a stone and throw it at her'.

Of course, nobody could pick up a stone.

I found these words inspiring because I could see they were true. Devotion is not the same as belief; it arises when something rings true to you. When something touches the core of your heart, you get inspired, and this leads to aspiration and certainty. This is true devotion.

Confusion Arises, p. 11-12.

Dusum Khyenpa's Experience of Certainty

The relationship between devotion and certainty.

The First Karmapa, Dusum Khyenpa, was a student of Gampopa. He was already an advanced practitioner when he met Gampopa. Even as a child, he was known for his clairvoyance. Later, he studied and practised in depth, and together with two men from Kham he went to central Tibet to become a student of Gampopa. Dusum Khyenpa practised in retreat for many years. After he felt he had a good understanding of the nature of the mind, he went to discuss his experience with Gampopa. However, Gampopa was not impressed. He told Dusum Khyenpa that his understanding was wrong, and to go back to his cave, try again, and meditate for another year.

Dusum Khyenpa went back into retreat and practised diligently. The next year he came back to see Gampopa, and he was in bad shape. He was unhappy and exhausted, and he told Gampopa that he was very sorry, but his experience of the nature of mind was the same as before. This time Gampopa became angry and shouted at him. He told Dusum Khyenpa that his experience was completely backward and not to come back until he had a definite experience of the mind's true nature.

Another year passed, and Dusum Khyenpa returned to see Gampopa again. He was crying and despondent, and he fell at Gampopa's feet, begging for further instructions because there was nothing he could do to change his experience. Even if Gampopa were to beat him or kill him, his experience wouldn't change; it was strong and clear. Then Gampopa smiled at him and congratulated him on his achievement. He said Dusum Khyenpa had been right all along, but it was extremely important for him to have conviction in the truth of his own experience.

This is an example of the kind of certainty involved in devotion.

Confusion Arises, p. 16.

IX

GREAT MASTERS

TILOPA AND NAROPA

The Vajrayana is not just about learning and teaching, there is something else, which could be called a heart to heart transmission.

Naropa was a very great scholar, one of the greatest of the five most important professors of the Nalanda University. At that time, it was the custom or the tradition, that anybody could challenge the doctrine in open debate, with the king of the country appointed witness and judge. Whoever lost the debate would become the follower of the winner. Therefore, at that time, to become a professor was much more difficult than now. Naropa was appointed 'Gate Keeper of the North'. He would debate with any challenger coming from the Northern direction of the University. He became very famous as one of the best scholars and he had many disciples.

One day, he was sitting in the sun on his veranda, reading a book, a very high tantric text. He was feeling very good about himself because he understood everything. Suddenly, a strange shadow fell on his book. He looked up and saw an ugly old lady standing beside him. She said, 'You do not understand anything of this!' Naropa was shocked and surprised, but realised at once that it was actually true: he understood the words, but not the experience.

He asked her, 'Who does understand?'

The old lady answered, 'My brother, Tilopa!' Leaving everything there, without even rolling up the text he was reading, Naropa left in search of Tilopa.

Eventually he found Tilopa and asked him to take him as a disciple, but Tilopa just stood up and walked away without even looking at him. Naropa followed him. This situation lasted for many years, during which Tilopa asked Naropa to do many completely crazy things. Finally, after undergoing many trials and hardships, coming close to death about thirteen times, Naropa received the transmission. It happened without a single word being uttered.

One day, as Naropa was walking towards him, Tilopa became very angry, took his sandal off and threw it at him. Naropa was hit on the head and fainted. When he came to, he knew everything that Tilopa knew, he had the complete experience. He had known everything before intellectually, but now he had the actual experience.

This may not be a very good example because it is so extreme. It does not mean that it should happen like that for all of us, but what this story illustrates is the fact that there is something else, not just the teachings, the texts and the understanding of their meaning; there is also the experience. True understanding is an experience. You may learn a lot from books and teachings, but it is still not enough. The guru is a medium to transmit that experience.

Ngöndro, p. 83; abbreviated variant *Daring Steps*, p. 181.

THE MONK WHO BROKE ONE OF HIS VOWS

What to do when you have done something wrong.

When Atisha Dipankara came to Tibet, he was asked by one of the monks, 'If I do something wrong and break one of my vows, what should I do?'

Atisha asked him, 'Where are you living now?'

The monk said he was living in retreat in a cave.

Atisha said, 'Okay, if you break a vow, go to Sangphu Monastery and publicly say, "I have broken this vow". Then go to Samye Monastery and again say to everyone, "I have broken this vow". Then go to Lhasa and say, "I have broken this vow". After that, go back to your retreat place and act as if you had never broken the vow'.

In other words, when you have done something wrong, you shouldn't agonise over it for the rest of your life. Dwelling on it doesn't help. We need to be realistic and keep our feet on the ground. It's important to form the resolve not to do the negative deed again, but it's also important to recognise that everyone makes mistakes.

Confusion Arises, p. 91.

Milarepa Benefits from his Students' Tsog

Milarepa, high up in the mountains in winter, is given up for lost.

Milarepa once went to a high snowy mountain to meditate. While he was up in his cave, snow started to fall heavily. It snowed for weeks and the path to the cave was completely blocked for the whole winter. Milarepa didn't have provisions for five or six months and his students were sadly convinced that their teacher had died, that there was no hope of seeing him again. They organised a ceremony for his death with prayers, *tsog pujas* [*tsog puja*: a ritual food offering], and other rituals. When spring came and the snow began to melt and the path was again accessible, the students went to the cave to get their master's dead body. They found Milarepa in the cave, but to their great surprise and delight, he was alive and even quite healthy. Milarepa told them that, on certain days, he had had the impression of eating a large and nourishing meal and had felt very comfortable.

These had been precisely the days when the students had organised the tsog pujas for him. Milarepa laughed and remarked that in this case, maybe tsog pujas were quite a good thing to do, because he had really felt as if he had eaten a lot.

The effectiveness of practice depends on the level of spiritual development of the practitioner, but also on the receptivity of the person for whom we are practising. It is also supposed to help in different subtle ways that are difficult to assess through our ordinary perceptions. Although not clearly or immediately visible, the effect may be there, at a deeper level.

Chenrezig, p. 94-95.

Gampopa Takes the Buddha's Teachings from India to Tibet

This and the following three stories are taken from a continuous text illustrating the importance for Buddhism, and for the Kagyu lineage in particular, of the life and teachings of Gampopa.

Gampopa was a special Bodhisattva during the time of Buddha Shakyamuni. One time when the Buddha was giving teachings about the future, he prophesied that his teaching would fade away in the Land of the Aryas, or India. It might be possible for his teachings to go north and flourish there, except that the people in the north behind the mountains were as difficult to penetrate as hard shells. The Buddha described them as barbarians, or the children of ogres. He must have been talking about the Tibetans, since we are supposed to be the offspring of a monster and an ogress.

Buddha went on to ask if any of the Bodhisattvas would be willing to go to such an unfavourable place with such difficult people. One particularly courageous Bodhisattva stood up and said, 'Yes, I will go there and spread the Dharma, no matter what'. After he spoke, five hundred other Bodhisattvas felt so inspired by his bravery that they stood up and said they would go to help him. It is said that Gampopa was the bravest Bodhisattva; he was the one who stood up first. Because of the strong promise he made to the Buddha, he became a great teacher who could benefit many beings. Not only that, but because many great Bodhisattvas were born in Tibet to help Gampopa, he created a very strong lineage.

Confusion Arises, p. 5.

GAMPOPA'S EARLY LIFE

Gampopa was born into a very good family, and he became a physician with a wife and two children. Not only was he a practising doctor, he also developed various medical treatments. Some of the medicines he created are still being used today.

What happened to change Gampopa's life was that his children died, and then his wife became terminally ill. Although her condition indicated she should be dead, she kept willing herself to stay alive. Gampopa said to her, 'You must have a very strong attachment to something, which is holding you back. Please tell me what it is so I can fulfil your wishes'.

She told him, 'I am not attached to anything in this world except you. I cannot bear to let you go'.

Then Gampopa told his wife that he had already decided to become a monk, whether or not she continued to live. He said he had seen enough of samsara, and he wanted to dedicate the rest of his life to practising the dharma and becoming enlightened. His wife asked him to take a vow in her presence that he would definitely renounce the world and become a monk. He agreed, and after he made this promise, she died.

The next morning, Gampopa's uncle came to see him. His uncle thought Gampopa would be devastated from the loss of his wife, but he found Gampopa in a cheerful frame of mind. His uncle became very angry with him for being so callous, but Gampopa assured him that he was happy because now he could devote himself totally to the Dharma. He was determined to become someone who could benefit a great number of beings.

Gampopa then divided his wealth into three parts: one part he distributed to the monasteries and the poor; one part he gave to the people practising on behalf of his wife; and one part he kept for his own expenses. Then Gampopa became a monk in the Kadampa tradition, which had been founded by the master

Atisha. Gampopa became very accomplished in the Kadampa teachings because he was very intelligent and already a very learned man.

Confusion Arises, p. 5-6.

Gampopa and the Beggars

While Gampopa was living at a Kadampa monastery, he started dreaming of a blue-coloured yogi coming to him, blessing him, and then going away. He dreamed this again and again, so he went to his teacher and asked his teacher what he thought this meant. His teacher told him, 'I don't know, but maybe it indicates a need to do retreat on Miyowa'. Miyowa, or Achala in Sanskrit, is a meditation deity with the ability to remove inner obstacles.

So Gampopa did a retreat on Miyowa while staying on the outskirts of the monastery. This was during a time of famine, and there were many beggars in the area. In particular, there were three beggars sleeping below a large rock near Gampopa. One day, one of the beggars said, 'I wish a sponsor would come to the monastery tomorrow and offer a very nice tsampa [roasted barley flour] soup, with big chunks of meat and bones, and invite everyone, including us. I really want some good soup'.

The second beggar said to the first, 'Don't think so small! Wish for something bigger than that. There is no harm in making a very big wish. You could wish to become the king of Tibet, like the great rulers of the past, Trisong Deutsen and Songtsen Gampo, who ruled over most of the world. They were powerful enough to attack China, and they brought the Dharma to Tibet. They did tremendous good for people. Wish for something like that. Aren't you ashamed of wishing for something as small as a cup of soup?'

Then the third man said, 'If you are going to make a wish, then wish for something better than being a king. Wish to be like Milarepa, who is completely free from samsara. He is totally enlightened and no longer has any need of food or clothing. He can fly from one village to another, and he teaches his students to become enlightened as well. Wish for something more like that. There is a retreatant up on that rock, and he usually circumambulates the monastery at this time of day. It would be embarrassing for him to hear us making such petty, worldly wishes'.

It turned out that indeed, at that very moment, Gampopa was walking by and heard this conversation. When he heard the name 'Milarepa', he became totally inspired. It was as if he had been struck by a thunderbolt. He had no doubt from that moment on that he should find Milarepa and study with him.

Confusion Arises, p. 6-7.

Gampopa Finds Milarepa

Gampopa had to make a long journey in order to meet Milarepa. Gampopa lived in central Tibet, and Milarepa lived far to the west, near Mount Kailash. Sometimes Gampopa got very sick on his journey, and Milarepa knew about this. Milarepa would tell his students, 'I can see my heart son coming. He is a great Bodhisattva who has incarnated to help Tibet by spreading the Dharma. He is on his way here, and now he is sick. Please pray for him'. Milarepa also told his students, 'Whoever brings this Bodhisattva to see me will never again be reborn in a lower realm, and instead will be quickly liberated'.

When Gampopa arrived at Milarepa's place, he met an old woman who asked him who he was and where he had come from. When he said he was a monk from central Tibet, she said, 'Oh, come in, come in! You must be the great Bodhisattva my teacher has been talking about. He said that whoever escorts you to him will have no more lower births, so please allow my daughter to take you to Milarepa'.

When Gampopa heard this, he thought, 'Oh, really! I must be someone special!' and he became a little proud. The next day, when the daughter took Gampopa to meet Milarepa, Milarepa wouldn't see him. Milarepa was aware of Gampopa's pride, and he kept Gampopa waiting for fifteen days.

When Milarepa finally granted him an audience, Gampopa prostrated in front of Milarepa, who was flanked by two other *repas*, or cotton-clad yogis, and then Gampopa sat down. Milarepa handed Gampopa a skull cup full of *chang*, or Tibetan liquor, and told Gampopa to drink it. Of course, monks are forbidden to drink alcohol, and Gampopa was a monk. But Gampopa did not hesitate; he took the skull cup and drank every drop. Milarepa was pleased by this and told Gampopa, 'You did very well. This is a sign that you will be a good vessel for my teachings'.

Milarepa gave him all the teachings and meditation instructions, and he worked closely with Gampopa on his meditative experiences. Actually, Gampopa wasn't with Milarepa for very long, but he did learn the Six Yogas of Naropa and Mahamudra, and gained experience in them. At a certain point, Milarepa said he had given Gampopa everything he had, like pouring liquid from one cup to another, and he said that Gampopa should go back to his homeland and practise there. He also said that when Gampopa finally considered his old teacher Milarepa to be no different from the Buddha himself, then Gampopa should start to teach.

The importance of Gampopa for Buddhism is immense. In terms of the way he taught, he combined the general Mahayana teachings he received from the Kadampa tradition of Atisha with the quintessential Vajrayana teachings, like the Six Yogas and Mahamudra, which he received from Milarepa. These became the basis of the Kagyu lineage teachings.

Confusion Arises, p. 7-8.

Atisha and the Short-tempered Monk

How to regard even those who are negative towards us, as our teacher.

Atisha, an eminent Indian pandit who lived in the eleventh century, was invited by the Tibetan king, Trisong Deutsen, to revive Buddhism in Tibet. When Atisha took up the king's invitation, he brought with him a monk who was the most awkward and short-tempered person imaginable. No matter what anyone said or did, invariably the monk became angry and spoiled the whole atmosphere.

People said to Atisha, 'You are such a compassionate and peaceful Lama. Why did you bring along this nasty man who is always fighting with everybody?'

Atisha replied, 'Oh, he is my teacher; he tests my patience'.

If, rather than getting angry, we can view someone who hurts us as a spiritual friend, his or her behaviour will turn into an instruction, giving us a lesson in patience. We should try to see things in this way.

Daring Steps, p. 88.

GREAT MASTERS

VIVEKANANDA AND THE ANGRY MAN

How to deal with anger and insults directed against us.

You may have heard of Vivekananda, an eminent Hindu teacher who lived during our era. One day he was travelling by train in India. Those who have been there know what Indian railways are like. At the station there are enormous crowds, and everyone pushes to get on. One time, when the train left, Vivekananda found himself stuck with an extremely angry man who shouted at him for a long time. All the time he was shouting, Vivekananda did not say a word. Finally, when the man was exhausted and could speak no more, Vivekananda calmly said, 'Suppose you give a present to someone and he does not accept it. With whom does the gift remain?'

'With the giver, of course', the man said.

Vivekananda replied, 'Yes, and I do not accept your insults'.

Someone who knows how to practise correctly sees the good in everybody, and tries to view others' negative actions as an instruction rather than an insult. So they do not need to react negatively to insults and can remain serene.

Daring Steps, p. 90; variant *Path to Buddhahood*, p. 52-3.

King Ashoka and the Man who Renounced Hatred

How to deal with hatred.

In his early years, the great Indian king Ashoka was very combative and waged war against his neighbouring countries, killing thousands of people. One day while travelling, he heard someone shouting, 'At last I have won. I am a great victor!' Ashoka ordered his men to find out what was happening. They found a man shouting by the bank of a river, into which he had thrown his sword.

They brought the man before the king, and Ashoka asked, 'Why are you making such a noise? What have you won?'

The man answered, 'For a long time I was filled with hatred. I had many enemies whom I tried to kill one by one. Eventually, I realised that for each enemy I killed another one arose, and as long as I nurtured hatred and the thirst for revenge within me, there would never be an end to my enemies. Since then I have been trying to overcome my anger, and I have finally succeeded. I have thrown my sword into the river. From today onward I will kill no more'.

His words kindled a spark in Ashoka's heart, and he thought, 'So, it can be done!' Later in his life Ashoka embraced non-violence, and played a major role in spreading Buddhism in Asia.

This story shows how we must work on our aversion. As long as our mind is filled with anger and revenge, everyone seems to be an enemy. Everything aggravates us and is viewed as being potentially harmful. However, the more our hatred decreases, the more our surroundings seem benign, since it is mainly our mind that determines what kind of experience we have.

Daring Steps, p. 93.

MILAREPA AND NYAMA PALDARBUM

Milarepa was the great Tibetan yogi celebrated for the 'Songs' in which
he crystallises his spiritual experience, and for his exemplary devotion to
the teachings of his master Marpa, for whom he underwent many trials
and tribulations, resulting in his final realisation. This story is a teaching
on the importance of stability within the movement of the mind.

Many people know the story of Nyama Paldarbum and Milarepa.
Milarepa gave these instructions to a woman who was one of his
disciples, whose name was Paldarbum:

'Meditate like the sky, without centre or limits. Meditate like the
sea, without bottom. Meditate like the mountain, with stability.'

So Paldarbum meditated for a while, then came back to see
Milarepa and said to him:

'It's very nice to meditate like the sky, but what do I do when there
are clouds passing in the sky? It's very good to meditate like the sea, but
what about the waves? It's very well to meditate when my mind is calm
and clear, but what should I do when thoughts and emotions arise?'

Then Milarepa told her, 'The clouds in the sky do not bother the
sky; they come and go without changing its nature. The waves are
no problem to the sea, as they are simply part of the sea. It is the
same for your mind. Thoughts and emotions should not bother you,
as they are part of your mind; they are just its natural manifestation'.

It's all a question of taking whatever arises as a part of the mind.
It comes and goes without causing disturbance. Joy, sadness, anger,
desire, insecurity, all thoughts and emotions just come and go. It's
okay. When you know that whatever comes will go anyway, you can
let it come; you are no longer overpowered by what arises.

Like Dreams and Clouds, p. 47-48.

INTEGRATION OF
DIFFERENT PRACTICES

How to bring the teachings you receive into your practice. And the importance of a genuine spiritual friend to guide this.

When the great Indian scholar Atisha arrived in Tibet, he asked his new students what they'd already studied. They gave him an impressive list of texts, treatises, tantras and so on. Atisha was pleased and a little surprised. 'You've already studied so much that my presence here is totally useless. You've already received all the teachings!' Then he asked, 'How do you practise what you have learned?'

They answered, 'We always practise according to what is said in each teaching, each tantra, sutra or text'. Atisha then understood the usefulness of his presence in Tibet.

If one doesn't know how to integrate the different practices into one, then all these teachings become a source of confusion. We shouldn't see them as separate elements but as supporting one another, like different facets of one and the same practice. A good teacher knows that all the Buddhist teachings are valid ways of working with the mind. The teacher sees how they fit together, and that there is no contradiction between them. Studying with a spiritual master who understands the teachings and knows how to practise them is therefore important. An appreciation of this will also create great devotion towards the teacher in the mind of the student.

Path to Buddhahood, p. 105; variant Confusion Arises, p. 13.

Milarepa, Rechungpa and the Yak Horn

Understanding the true nature of things. From a Buddhist point of view, even time and space are relative and have no fixed, solid existence. Different events can simultaneously take place in the same space.

This is illustrated by the story of Milarepa and the yak horn. Milarepa had a student called Rechungpa. Tibet is a very cold country, but Milarepa had mastered the yogic technique of inner heat [*tummo*]and he was wearing just one piece of cotton cloth even in the high mountains of the Himalayas. His student could do the same but he was smaller than Milarepa, which is why he was called Rechungpa. *Re* means 'cotton' in Tibetan, and *chung* means 'small'. He was the 'Small Cotton-Clad One'. Milarepa had sent him to India to bring back teachings he hadn't yet received.

Rechungpa came back with those teachings, but he had also brought back some books of black magic. Milarepa, who had come to welcome him on his way back, knew this and wanted to destroy those books that would only harm Rechungpa. He burned them while Rechungpa was fetching water, but when Rechungpa learned this, he got very angry and resented Milarepa for having done so. On the ensuing trip back, he was walking behind his teacher, sulking.

They had to cross a big plateau where nothing grew and there was no shelter. A yak horn lay on the ground, and Milarepa told Rechungpa to take it, that it might be useful soon. Rechungpa did so, grudgingly, thinking that his teacher had gone crazy, destroying valuable things and collecting worthless ones. When they reached the centre of the plateau, a violent hailstorm broke out. Milarepa asked Rechungpa to put the horn on the ground and he quickly went into the horn for shelter. The horn didn't grow big and Milarepa didn't shrink. He just sat comfortably inside the horn, singing a song inviting Rechungpa to join him inside. How could this happen? How can one sit inside a yak horn without the horn growing any bigger or one becoming any smaller?

Such seemingly impossible things can happen when one has the full understanding of the true nature of things.

Path to Buddhahood, p. 122-123.

MILAREPA'S FIRST
ENCOUNTER WITH THE
DHARMA

The practice of meditation.

Maybe you know the story of Milarepa's first encounter with the Dharma? He had asked a Lama for instructions so as to practise the Dharma. The Lama told him, 'You're really lucky! You've knocked at the right door! I have a very strong and direct method. If you start to meditate in the morning, you'll get enlightened in the afternoon. If you start meditating in the afternoon, you'll get enlightened the next morning'.

Convinced that he was really lucky – because he had previously been immediately successful in studying black magic – Milarepa didn't bother to start practising at once. A few days later, the Lama came to enquire how he was doing. Milarepa told him that he hadn't even started, because he thought he could reach his goal any time. The Lama then sighed and explained that this wasn't what he had meant. He had to send him to another teacher because his instructions would now be useless for Milarepa.

Let's avoid such a mistake!

Path to Buddhahood, p. 127- 128.

Milarepa's Secret Teaching to Gampopa

The experiential methods of the Vajrayana, as opposed to mere intellectual understanding.

Milarepa's best disciple was Gampopa. After he had received all the necessary instructions and gained genuine experience of them, Milarepa told him to go to a mountain called 'Gampodar' near the Nepalese border where he would find his disciples. When Gampopa was ready to leave, Milarepa accompanied him part of the way, until they had reached a small stream.

Here Milarepa said, 'Now you go, my son'. Then he hesitated and said, 'I have not given you my most secret instruction, though... but maybe I should not do so either'.

Gampopa prostrated himself many times, offered a mandala and did everything to request the teaching, but he finally had to turn and go on his way.

After he had crossed the water and reached the far bank, Milarepa called him back and said, 'After all, you are my best disciple! If I do not give this teaching to you, to whom else should I give it?' Gampopa was filled with joy and prostrated himself over and over again, expecting a very sublime and outstanding instruction. Then Milarepa turned around and, lifting his clothes, showed Gampopa his backside. It was covered with innumerable scars from meditating sitting on rocks for so long.

He said, 'Look, my son. This is my final and most secret instruction!'

This shows the importance for ourselves of actually practising the instructions of Dharma and meditation. This was Milarepa's final and innermost teaching to his heart-son.

Daring Steps, p. 20; variant *Path to Buddhahood*, p. 131.

X

CRAZY WISDOM

DO KHYENTSE

Stories about the great tantric yogi Do Khyentse, illustrating his unconventional character.

STORY I:

One day, Do Khyentse was staying near Dzogchen Monastery. As with most Buddhist monks, especially from Tibet, the monks there were somewhat sceptical and did not easily believe anything. Hearing that the renowned Do Khyentse was in the neighbourhood, two of them decided to play a trick on him. 'Look at this fool', they said, 'he doesn't have any understanding whatsoever. Let's put him to a test!'

Then one of them lay down in the road pretending to be dead, while the other ran up to Do Khyentse in apparent distress crying, 'Khyentse Rinpoche, Khyentse Rinpoche, please come with me! My friend has just fallen down and died! Please perform *phowa* [the transference of consciousness] for him!'

Do Khyentse turned his horse and followed him back. When they reached the 'corpse', he rapped his pipe on the monk's head three times, knocking out the ashes, and said, 'All right, it is done,' and left.

Then the other monk said to his friend, 'You see, we were right. He is totally stupid. He can't even tell the dead from the living. Get up and let's go'. His friend, however, did not get up. No matter how much he shook him, he did not move. Aghast, he realised that his friend was really dead.

Now, he was very frightened and, full of remorse, ran back after Do Khyentse, and in tears begged him, 'Please forgive me, we were just testing you. Please come back and revive my friend'.

Khyentse said, 'Is it true? He was not dead?'

The monk answered, 'No, he was not. We just pretended to put you to a test'.

At this Do Khyentse replied, 'All right, if this is so', and once more went back with the monk to where the other was still lying in the road dead. Again, three times he knocked out the ashes of his pipe on the monk's head and rode away.

Then the dead monk arose and complained to his friend, 'Why did you ask him to bring me back? I was feeling so good in the pure realms!'

STORY II:

Another time, three monks went to see Do Khyentse and asked him to accept them as his disciples. He said he would, provided they abandoned their guru for him. Otherwise, he told them, he would not grant any teaching. 'Think about it well overnight,' he said, 'and if tomorrow you are ready to give up your guru, come back and I will give you teaching. If not, I will send you away'.

The following morning two of the monks said to each other, 'Well, it is maybe for some auspicious reason that he talked like that. It does not mean that we really have to give up our guru. Let's go and receive his teachings anyway'.

The third said, 'No, I already have my guru, who has given me ample instructions. I will not forsake him in order to get further teachings I do not need.' Whereupon, he left.

The other two went to see Do Khyentse and asked him for teaching. He looked intently at them and said, 'So you are truly willing to give up your guru?'

They both said, 'Yes, we are'.

He asked them where their companion went, and they told him that he could not accept the condition and instead had gone away. Hearing that, Do Khyentse took whatever dirt lay in front of him and threw it into their faces, shouting, 'You fools! You think I would give instruction to a student who would abandon his teacher? Go immediately in search of your friend who has left and bring him to me. I want to see him'.

When the friend was brought back, Do Khyentse said that he had acted rightly. Subsequently, he kept him as his assistant. Sometimes he instructed him, but mainly he took him wherever he went and gave him a lot of trouble as well. After Do Khyentse had passed away, this disciple, popularly known as Aku Özer, assumed the task of compiling and editing the greatest part of his works.

STORY III

Do Khyentse's main teacher was the first Dodrubchen. And Do Khyentse's main student was Patrul Rinpoche, who later composed the famous text known as *The Words of My Perfect Teacher*. When he met Do Khyentse, Patrul Rinpoche was already a very learned scholar and highly respected for his intellect. His main teacher had been a great khenpo, called Nyushu Lungtog. In his younger days, Patrul Rinpoche was quite active in worldly affairs. He was a good negotiator and had a very strong personality. At times, he was maybe even a little proud.

In one encounter, Patrul Rinpoche had camped nearby where Do Khyentse was camped. One day, Do Khyentse came along on his horse in a combative mood and shouted at Patrul Rinpoche, 'Hey, Palge Tulku, you old dog! You think you are really great? You are nothing! I challenge you. If you are brave, come here and fight with me!'

Patrul Rinpoche thought to himself, 'He is such a great teacher but must be drunk and confused to be acting like this'.

Do Khyentse came nearer and said, 'You think I'm drunk? You think you're so great?' With that, he grabbed Patrul Rinpoche's hair and tossed him about, dragging him around, shouting, 'You are a dog! You are nothing but a wretched dog!

If you have any guts, get on your feet and fight with me!' With that he beat him up.

Later Patrul Rinpoche said that this was the greatest introduction to the nature of his mind. Before, he had some recognition and understanding, but it was only like the dawn of a day. This, then, was like the radiance of the mid-day sun.

Thereafter, he always considered Do Khyentse as his teacher and called himself 'the tattered old dog', especially when composing a Vajrayana text. He would say, 'This is my secret name, my tantric name, given to me by my master'.

Do Khyentse's behaviour may have looked unconventional and even crazy, but it gave his students the greatest teachings, cutting through all vestiges of ego-clinging.

Daring Steps, p. 120-22; variant of Story I: *Path to Buddhahood*, p. 36-37.

DRUKPA KUNLEY

A discussion of various types of empowerment and ways to teach.

STORY I:

Drukpa Kunley was a seemingly crazy yogi who never meditated in the conventional fashion, not even for a single day. He just wandered around the country and appeared to be mischievously fooling about and doing things that weren't totally respectable. For this reason, he was a source of continuous offense to his brother, who was his total opposite, a very proper and learned monk whose behaviour was always impeccable. Yet, despite his outward appearance, Drukpa Kunley was a highly enlightened being.

Becoming increasingly annoyed with Drukpa Kunley's activities, his brother finally had enough, and said to him, 'You act like a madman! This has to stop – you are a disgrace to Buddhism. You must withdraw into seclusion and meditate with me for at least a few months'. With these words, he forcefully took Drukpa Kunley to his retreat place and told him to meditate in the adjoining room. To please him, Drukpa Kunley did as he was told.

His brother was sitting in his room solemnly immersed in meditation, but soon his gaze fell on a white yak tail hanging from the ceiling and he began to day-dream, thinking, 'Next time I go to Lhasa, I will take this nice yak tail with me and have it dyed red. Then, I will decorate my mule with it!' It was the custom in Tibet to fasten a red yak tail to the head of a mule and hang a big bell around its neck. A caravan of these mules was a very impressive sight.

No sooner had this thought passed through his mind than his attendant knocked at his door. Slightly indignant, Drukpa Kunley's brother enquired, 'What is it? Do not disturb me. I am in meditation'.

The attendant said, 'I'm sorry. But this is very urgent. Your brother has just run away. He suddenly jumped up and left for Lhasa'.

Drukpa Kunley's brother was outraged and cried, 'This is going too far. He cannot leave the retreat like that! Go immediately and send some people to bring him back!'

The attendant did as he was told, and as soon as Drukpa Kunley was brought back, his brother scolded him, 'What do you think you are doing? We were meant to be in retreat for several months. How can you run away like that?'

Drukpa Kunley replied in an astonished tone, 'I thought the retreat was over'.

Unable to believe his ears, his brother exclaimed, 'Where did you get that idea? This is just another of your follies!'

Drukpa Kunley said, 'Not at all. When I saw you go to Lhasa to have that yak tail dyed red, I thought the retreat was finished!'

Daring Steps, p. 138-39; variant *Path to Buddhahood*, p. 101-102.

STORY II:

Being such a proper Lama in every respect, Drukpa Kunley's brother also possessed a set of very precious ritual implements. Made of silver and gold and manufactured with sublime handicraft, they were very dear to his heart. One day, Drukpa Kunley paid a visit to his brother's camp and said, 'Today I have to request something very significant from you. I have to give an empowerment of utmost importance to my reputation. Would you lend me your ritual objects for just one day?'

His brother was very suspicious and said, 'You have never given any initiations. What is this supposed to be now?'

Drukpa Kunley replied, 'You are right. But today is a special occasion, and this empowerment is really very important. I must give it'.

'What is it called?' his brother enquired.

'Its name is "Untying the Knot of Miserliness",' said Drukpa Kunley.

CRAZY WISDOM

At this, his brother grew even more suspicious. 'I have never heard of any such initiation,' he said, 'you are joking'.

Drukpa Kunley insisted, 'No, please. There is an initiation called "Untying the Knot of Miserliness", and I must definitely give it'.

Finally his brother gave in. 'If this is so', he said, 'I will lend you my ritual objects, but please take care of them and make sure they are not damaged'.

Drukpa Kunley promised. 'Don't worry, I will secure them on my back and guard them with my life.' Reluctantly, his brother handed him the box with the ritual objects. Drukpa Kunley fastened it on his back and immediately set out for a nearby mountain and started to climb. As soon as he reached the top, he let himself fall and rolled down its steep slope.

When his brother's attendants saw this, they cried, 'Come quickly! Your brother has fallen down the mountain'. Drukpa Kunley's brother was deeply upset. Thinking that Drukpa Kunley had met with an accident, they all ran to where he was lying.

'What has happened? What has happened?' his brother cried, 'Are you hurt?'

'I'm not hurt,' Drukpa Kunley replied, 'but look, all your precious objects are totally ruined. I'm so very sorry.'

His brother was relieved that he was unharmed. 'Oh, don't worry about that,' he said, 'it's all right. As long as you're not hurt, it does not matter.' In this way, he received Drukpa Kunley's empowerment, 'Untying the Knot of Miserliness'.

Daring Steps, p. 139-40.

STORY III:

The story goes that at one time there was a drought near Lhasa. It had not rained for months and everything was drying up. Various Lamas did pujas and rituals, but nothing seemed to help. Finally, people asked Drukpa Kunley, 'Can't you do something? You are supposed to be a realised yogi'.

He told them, 'I can help you, but you must do exactly what I say'.

They agreed to do whatever he asked. He said he wanted all the monks of the three big monasteries – Ganden, Drepung, and Sera – to assemble at a certain place and to bring with them a great deal of *tsampa*, or roasted barley flour.

When the monks came, Drukpa Kunley took off all his clothes until he was completely naked. He stood on his head and told the monks to put the tsampa on his buttocks. As they were piling on the tsampa, he started farting, and the tsampa billowed up in the air, making a big cloud with a very bad smell. The cloud went higher and higher, and grew larger and larger, and then it began to rain.

Confusion Arises, p. 162.

The activity of a realised yogi may go beyond the socially conventional where necessary, because they are beyond caring about how they themselves look, and care only about helping others. Generally speaking, we sometimes need a shock to the mind, rather than words, for us to reach the point of seeing things clearly. In the first story here, this clarity leads us to see that there is not necessarily a fixed routine in which empowerment is transmitted; it can be done in any manner. For those who have an affinity for ceremony and who attach great importance to outer form, empowerment can be conveyed in a very elaborate and ritualised manner. For a disciple who does not have this tendency or has an adverse affinity, the teacher can just use the environment, or even no outer support at all.

XI

RIGHT THOUGHT
AND RIGHT ACTION

THE MOTHER BIRD AND HER CHICKS

The importance of right thought, and cultivating the right habitual tendencies in order to act positively.

A mother bird nested in a field and hatched her chicks. When the chicks had come out of the shell, the mother went away every day to fetch food and came back in the evening. One day, she found her children deeply worried. In a great flurry they told her, 'We have to leave immediately. We are in great danger! The farmer has been here with his son. They said they want to reap the grain tomorrow, so they are getting all their neighbours in the village to help them'.

The mother reassured them, 'Don't worry, just sit here quietly. Nothing will happen'. The next day, she went out as usual and her words proved to be true.

Upon her return, again the chicks were very excited and told her, 'The farmer and his son have been here once more and said they will now harvest the grain tomorrow. Since none of their neighbours had time, they are going to ask all their relatives for help'.

Again the mother soothed them and said, 'Don't be anxious. Nothing will happen'. When she returned the following day, the chicks were quite calm and relaxed. She had been right again. Nothing had happened. They told her, though, that the farmer and his son had been round again and had mentioned that, since the grain still needed to be cut and since their relatives did not have time either, they would do it on their own the following day.

Hearing this, the mother was alerted and said, 'Get ready, we are no longer safe here. We will leave as soon as we can'.

The mother bird had the wisdom to see the situation clearly, and what action was needed. Just as the chicks learn wise conduct through the thoughts and actions of their mother, so we can gradually reform our thoughts, which are the starting-point for all our actions. Our thoughts determine whether we act in a right or wrong way, as well as what kind of person we become.

Daring Steps, p. 40-41.

XII

MEDITATION
PRACTICE

The Efficacy of Mantras

STORY I:

Atisha [Dipankara] was a most learned Indian Pandit who was invited to Tibet in the 11th century. He developed a throat problem due to the harsh Tibetan climate and the altitude, and he couldn't get rid of the infection for a long time. Somebody mentioned a Tibetan who had helped many people by saying mantras, and Atisha agreed to see him.

This Tibetan man was brought in, who recited the mantras very loudly, with very good intentions; but, because he was Tibetan, he didn't pronounce them properly. Atisha Dipankara was so bemused to hear the mantras pronounced in such a completely wrong way that he couldn't help laughing. He laughed and laughed, and he laughed so much that eventually the infectious blister in his throat burst open and he was cured!

Chenrezig, p. 37.

STORY II:

There's another funny story about fake mantras. A man once asked a so-called Lama to teach him a mantra. However, that Lama was just posing as a Lama and didn't actually know anything. The man was earnestly requesting a mantra and the fake Lama didn't know what to say. Embarrassed, he looked around and saw a mouse appearing suddenly from a hole in the wall. He then said in Tibetan, 'Pop up suddenly'. He saw the mouse's whiskers and added, 'It has whiskers'. And then, as the mouse ran to and fro, searching and scratching around, he added, 'It rummages here and there'. Finally the mouse disappeared, so he said, 'It disappears'. And then, 'There you are, that's the mantra'.

The man thanked the fake Lama and went away, reciting his freshly learnt mantra on the way. On his way home he had to travel through a dangerous place infested with robbers. He had to camp there for the night and he was terrified. Hoping the mantra would protect him, he recited it loudly. One of the robbers caught sight of him and decided to rob and kill him. The brigand slowly crawled to the tent. He was very near it when he heard a voice saying, 'Pop up suddenly'. Surprised, he thought the man was aware of his arrival. He stopped and listened more carefully. 'It has whiskers'. This thief had whiskers: he now really wondered whether the man knew of his presence. Then he started hunting about to see whether he could get hold of something outside the tent, and he heard, 'It rummages here and there'. By now, the thief was convinced that this man had special powers and knew about his presence and intentions. He was getting really scared and wondering what to do. Then he heard, 'It disappears'. So he ran away.

So the fake mantra worked quite well in a way. And of course the man who recited it had total confidence in his mantra and its efficacy.

Mantra-recitation, even if seemingly fake, can have surprising and unintended results. This comes about through the interdependence of the words said, the state of mind of the person saying them and many other factors.

Chenrezig, p. 38.

MEDITATION PRACTICE

STORY III:

Sakya Pandita, a Tibetan master who lived around the 12th century (1182-1251), was not only a great scholar but also a highly realised practitioner. Although he was never taught Sanskrit, it was the first language he could speak as a small child. He became a great Sanskrit scholar. He used to travel to India to debate with Indian philosophers and he converted many Hindus to Buddhism.

Once, as he was travelling from Tibet to India, he was passing through a dense forest. He could hear the sounds of mantras emanating from all over the place – from the trees, the rivers and the rocks. He thought that a great practitioner must be living nearby. However, the sound of the mantra he was hearing was not completely correct and he thought, 'What a pity! If this yogi is able to give such power to an incorrect mantra, how much more power it would have if he were saying it correctly!' So he searched around to find the yogi. Having found him, he introduced himself, paid his respects, praised him for his great achievement and suggested that he pronounce the mantra in the right way.

'You're saying "*Om bendza chili chilaya...*" whereas it's supposed to be "*Om vajra kili kilaya...*". You should change it.'

The yogi then took his *phurba* [or *kilaya*, a ritual dagger], and recited '*Om bendza chili chilaya...*' and struck a rock with the dagger. It went through the rock as if through butter. He turned to Sakya Pandita: 'Now, please, you do the same with *kili kilaya*!' But Sakya Pandita did not try.

The power of a mantra does not necessarily depend on how 'correctly' it is recited, but on the degree of realisation of the reciter.

Chenrezig, p. 46-47.

Prayer Recitation

A story about reciting prayers, in this case, Christian prayers.

A bishop once visited three monks who lived on an island. The three monks were happy to welcome the bishop. The bishop asked them what kind of prayers they were saying. The three men answered that they worshipped God from the bottom of their heart, but that the only prayer they knew was: 'You three, we three, please bless us!'

'Oh no! That's not the right prayer. You must learn how to pray properly!' exclaimed the bishop.

With great enthusiasm, the three monks begged him to teach them how to pray. 'We're so grateful that you have come to teach us.' Then the bishop taught them the Lord's Prayer: *'Our Father who art in Heaven...'*.

Unfortunately, it was very hard for the three men to learn it by heart. The bishop, who was a very nice person, patiently kept on repeating it and spent a long time teaching them until, at last, all of them could say the prayer nicely. Then he bid them farewell, went back to his boat and sailed away.

The next morning, as he stood on the deck, he saw three luminous points on the horizon; they seemed to be moving towards the boat. As they drew near, the bishop recognised the three monks, who were running on the waves. They were shouting, 'Please, please, stop! Please tell us the prayer once more because we have forgotten it'.

Quite stunned, the bishop told them that he thought they no longer needed his prayer and that they could simply go on saying their own prayer: 'You three, we three, please bless us'. It seemed to be working just fine!

Faith is more important than doing 'the correct thing'.

Chenrezig, p. 47-48.

A SHOOTING CONTEST

Archery is used as an illustration to compare being a crack shot and an accomplished meditator.

In this story, a great master had been teaching the Kauravas and the Pandava brothers to shoot arrows. The master organised a test to determine who his best student was. He put a small clay figure of a bird in a tree and asked each of his students to aim at it. They were all very good shots.

'What can you see?' he asked the first one.

'I see the leaves and the bird in the middle.' The teacher did not let him shoot. He put the same question to the next one.

'I can see the bird, nothing else.' He didn't let him shoot either.

One of the strongest students said, 'I can see just the head of the bird'. But he, too, was refused the opportunity to shoot. Finally, Arjuna's turn came.

'What can you see?' asked the master.

'I can see only the eye of the bird, nothing else.'

'Now you shoot!' The arrow pierced the clay bird's eye, and Arjuna was proclaimed the best student.

When one is very concentrated, the mind is very focused and one sees only the object on which the mind is settled. This is good in the beginning, but it's not the whole thing in meditation. One also has to be aware of everything going on around, of all the five senses open and reacting, but at the same time one must maintain clarity and calmness.

Chenrezig, p. 50-51.

GESHE BEN

*The importance of mindfulness in our efforts to help all
sentient beings.*

There is a famous story about Geshe Ben, a Tibetan practitioner
who used to say, 'I do not carry out any practice other than
looking at my mind'.

One day Geshe Ben was informed that some of his devotees
were coming to see him. He cleaned his place carefully and
prepared a table with abundant offerings. Then he sat down
and asked himself, 'What am I doing and why am I doing it?'
When he found that he intended to impress his devotees and
was hoping for their praise, he immediately went to the fireplace,
took a handful of ashes and threw them on his shrine. Then he sat
down again and waited for his visitors. Word of what he had done
spread, eventually reaching the ears of Atisha Dipamkara, who
said, 'That was the best offering he could possibly make'.

At another time Geshe Ben was staying with a family in
a village. He wanted to go into retreat in a cave, but had very
little tsampa, the barley flour that is the traditional staple food in
Tibet. However, the family had a big supply, and when nobody
was around he thought, 'Why not take a bit of their tsampa with
me? They have so much and I have nothing'. He fetched his
tsampa bag and put his right hand into the family's big sack. At
that moment he realised what he was doing. With his left hand he
seized his right hand inside the sack and shouted at the top of his
voice, 'A thief has come! Thief! Thief!' Everybody came running
and asked, 'What is happening? Where is the thief?' Geshe Ben
showed his right hand and said, 'Here he is!'

*This shows how we should try to catch ourselves and see whether what
we are doing is right or wrong. If we understand that we are not doing*

MEDITATION PRACTICE

the right thing and another course of action would be better, not only for ourselves but for everybody else, we should behave accordingly. That is how we create a positive habit. This is a key practice, which is done, not only for a limited time, but throughout our lives.

Daring Steps, p. 112-113.

The Man who was Reborn as an Evil Spirit

Creation Stage practice; stability and compassion.

There is a Tibetan story about a man who had done a lot of Creation Stage practice [meditating on a visualised form] and thus developed great stability. However, he lacked compassion, and so after he died he was reborn as an evil spirit.

One time this evil spirit appeared as a very negative vision to a sincere Lama who was in retreat in a cave. The Lama recognised the spirit as merely a negative vision, and he decided to exorcise it. The Lama was also a very stable practitioner. He visualised himself as a wrathful deity and said wrathful mantras. But the evil spirit was able to visualise himself as an even more wrathful deity, and he said even more powerful mantras back to the Lama.

It became clear to the Lama that this spirit knew how to do Creation Stage practice, and that the spirit must have once been a strong practitioner who somehow went the wrong way . Seeing this made the Lama very sad, and he felt genuine compassion for the spirit. He thought, 'What a pity! This person must have done so much practice and spent so much time in retreat. And this is what he has come to be. How unfortunate!'

While the Lama was thinking this, he forgot about visualising and saying mantras, and just felt this natural, strong compassion. He looked up and saw that the vision was becoming smaller and smaller and dissolving away. As the vision was disappearing, he heard it say in a very quiet voice, 'This is exactly what I did not have'. In other words, the spirit recognised that what he was missing was compassion.

A stable Creation Stage practice can make your mind very strong, particularly through the training of mantras. But a stable mind alone cannot liberate you. Along with stability, Creation Stage practice also needs wisdom and compassion.

Confusion Arises, p. 113.

THE MEDITATING MONKEYS

Importance of the physical posture in meditation.

There is a story in the sutras in which a group of monkeys were watching some *arhats* [accomplished practitioners] meditating in the woods. Later these monkeys were seen meditating in the same posture. Through this, they actually attained the stability of mind known as *shiné* in the Tibetan tradition.

The posture of the body affects the mind in many ways. Once the physical posture is correct, its effect on the mind will be very positive.

Daring Steps, p. 45.

XIII

KARMA

THE LAST WISH OF THE CRIMINAL SENTENCED TO DEATH

A teaching about karma.

Once there was a criminal who was sentenced to death. When asked if he had a last wish before his execution, he said he wanted to meet his mother one more time. When his mother came, they were both very moved. When he hugged her, it looked like he was going to kiss her, but actually he bit her nose.

Everyone was shocked and wanted to know why he did that. The man said that he became a criminal because of his mother's behaviour. When he was a child, he used to bring home pieces of chalk from school. His mother would praise him, saying he was so clever for taking the chalk. Then, he started to bring home pencils and books, and she was even more pleased. He said he knew he was stealing, but instead of rebuking and disciplining him, his mother encouraged him. At first he was a petty thief, but he became a bigger thief and a bigger criminal, until he reached the point where he was sentenced to death for his crimes.

Even the tiniest actions can ripen into big obstacles. Something can start off rather harmless, but it can ripen into something very negative.

Confusion Arises, p. 26-27.

Questions of Karma

The interaction of all the actions we make, is complex.

An old woman had just listened to the teachings about the results of karma at the nearby monastery. Talking about the benefits of positive action, the Lama had claimed that even a sham positive action would have great results and that, for example, thanks to a single recitation of the name of Buddha Amitabha, one would be reborn in the pure land of Sukhavati. Speaking about the negative effects of bad actions, he had said that the smallest error, even a simple lie, was enough to plunge one into the hells for thousands of cosmic eons. The old woman, perplexed, went to the Lama and asked him, 'If what you said about the results of good deeds is true, not only Lamas but even I won't fail to become Buddha in this life. On the other hand, if I believe what you said about bad actions, not only I but even you will surely go to hell! So where do we stand?'

In fact, none of us behaves completely positively or negatively. Our behaviour, our karmas are composed of so many mismatched elements all bound up together, the negative with the positive, that the results are also extremely complex.

Path to Buddhahood, p. 44-45.

KING AJATASHATRU LIBERATES HIMSELF FROM THE CHAIN OF KARMA

A teaching on liberating ourselves by breaking the chain of karma: conquering our ignorance and confusion liberates us from the illusion of ego.

During the Buddha's lifetime, the king Ajatashatru killed his father, who was a holy arhat. Later, under the influence of Devadatta, a jealous cousin of the Buddha, he himself attempted to kill the Buddha. Luckily, he wasn't able to commit this heinous act.

The years went by and he came to understand the horror of his crimes. Full of remorse, he repented and begged the Buddha to send him someone to hear his confession and help him to purify himself. The Buddha sent him Manjushri who, instead of reassuring him, promised him the blackest hell, without the least hope of release.

Ajatashatru was desperate. When he reached the very deepest despair, Manjushri asked him suddenly, 'Look closely. Who is going to burn in hell? What, in you, will really be going to hell? What, or who?' Ajatashatru looked and thereupon, in an instant, realised his true nature.

Ajatashatru saw that he was not an independent unit that would go to hell, but an aggregate and an arising from many causes and conditions in a constant state of flux; almost a process. In an instant, he had realised his own true nature. In an instant, he had broken the karmic chain and liberated himself completely. He had reached the first level of realisation.

Path to Buddhahood, p. 48-49.

THE STORY OF VALMIKI

A teaching about how our own karma is only ours, and belongs to nobody else. Nobody can share the burden of any bad karma we create, it is our responsibility.

Valmiki is said to be the first poet of India, and lived a long, long time ago. It so happens that he was a robber, a highwayman. He would sit in wait in the forest and rob anybody who passed by. One day he was waiting in the woods when he spotted a *rishi*, a person dedicated to a spiritual path.

Valmiki stopped him and demanded, 'Give me everything, otherwise I will kill you!'

The rishi responded, 'Well, I have nothing, but you can take whatever you like. But why are you doing this, why are you like this? Why are you not working or doing something else?'

Valmiki replied, 'I am doing this because of my family, to support my family and to support my parents. Anyway, it is none of your business. You just give me everything'.

The rishi said, 'It is all right. I will give you everything. I really don't have that much, but you can take everything. But tell me, why are you doing this negative and bad thing for your family, your children and parents? It is not nice'.

Valmiki replied, 'This is my profession. I do this for all of them'.

The rishi continued, 'But then you have lots of bad karma by doing these negative things... I am sure your parents are not going to share your bad karma. Your wife is not going to share your bad karma. Your children are not going to share your bad karma. They would all be ashamed'.

At this, Valmiki became very angry. 'No, you are wrong! They are going to share my bad karma because I am only doing this for them.'

The rishi replied, 'No, I am sure that they will not share your karma. You just go back and ask them whether they are willing to share your bad karma or not'.

Valmiki answered, 'Well, you will run away during that time'.

But the rishi responded, 'No, no, just bind me to the tree'.

Valmiki tied the rishi to the tree and went to ask his father, 'You know, I am doing lots of negative things to get food for the family. It might have a negative result in the next life. Are you going to share that?'

And his father said, 'Oh no, no, no! I am not going to share any of that. I am very old. I am dying now. You are supposed to feed us and look after the family and the way you do it is up to you. Your bad karma is your responsibility and I cannot share it with you even if I wanted to'.

Next, Valmiki went to his mother and she reacted in a similar way. Immediately, he went to his wife but she too was not ready to share his bad karma. Then he went to his children and they were even less ready to share his bad karma.

Valmiki was very shocked. Returning to the rishi, he untied him and said, 'What you said is true. They are not willing to share my bad karma. So, what shall I do?'

To this the rishi replied, 'Oh, you can do whatever you like, you can carry on as you are or you can practise, you can purify your bad karma'.

Valmiki said, 'All right, what is it that I should be doing? You teach me how to meditate and I am going to practise'.

So the rishi taught him how to meditate and Valmiki sat under a tree and meditated. He was such a strong man, such a determined person, that once he began to meditate he soon went into *samadhi* [meditative absorption].

Slowly, slowly, over time, the ants came and built an anthill over his body. Then, after I don't know how many months or how many years, when he came back to consciousness, he looked around and saw that his entire body was covered by the anthill. There were only two small holes through which he could look out. Through the holes he saw two birds peacefully gliding in the sky. Valmiki felt so good and so joyful that he uttered a verse that is said to be the first stanza of the great Indian epic, the *Ramayana*, which he later composed.

We must take responsibility for our own actions: whether good or bad, we will reap the benefits or obstacles they create. Through strong practice, purification of bad karma is possible.

Dealing with Emotions, p. 8-10.

XIV

FEAR AND AVERSION

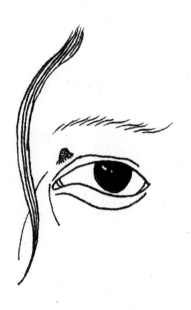

THE PRINCESS WITH THE EYE PROBLEM

The broad view of a Bodhisattva, compared with our usual narrow focus on our own small problems.

There is a story about a princess who had a small eye problem that she felt was really bad. Being the king's daughter, she was rather spoiled and kept crying all the time. When the doctors wanted to apply medicine, she would invariably refuse any medical treatment and kept touching the sore spot on her eye. In this way it became worse and worse, until finally the king proclaimed a large reward for whoever could cure his daughter. After some time, a man arrived who claimed to be a famous physician, but actually was not even a doctor. He declared that he could definitely cure the princess and was admitted to her chamber. After he had examined her, he exclaimed, 'Oh, I'm so sorry!' 'What is it?' the princess enquired. The doctor said, 'There's nothing much wrong with your eye, but there is something else that is really serious'. The princess was alarmed and asked, 'What on earth is so serious?' He hesitated and said, 'It is really bad. I shouldn't tell you about it'. No matter how much she insisted, he refused to tell her, saying that he could not speak without the king's permission.

When the king arrived, the doctor was still reluctant to reveal his findings. Finally the king commanded, 'Tell us what is wrong. Whatever it is, you have to tell us!' At last the doctor said, 'Well, the eye will get better within a few days – that's no problem. The big problem is that the princess will grow a tail, which will become at least nine fathoms long. It may start growing very soon. If she can detect the first moment it appears, I might be able to prevent it from growing'. At this news everyone was deeply concerned. And the princess, what did she do? She stayed in bed, day and night, directing all her attention to detect when the tail might appear. Thus, after a few days, her eye got well. But she did not grow a tail.

When she asked the man, 'Why isn't a tail growing?' he enquired instead, 'Oh, your eye is all right?'

'Yes, my eye is all right. But what about the tail?'

'Actually I had to divert your attention and stop you touching your eye all the time, in order to allow your eye to heal', he responded. 'No tail is going to grow.'

This shows how we usually react. We focus on our little problem and it becomes the centre around which everything else revolves. So far, we have done this repeatedly, life after life. As long as we function on this basis, we will remain unchanged. Driven by impulses of desire and rejection, we will travel the roads of samsara without finding a way out. As long as attachment and aversion control our lives and drive us onward, we cannot rest.

Daring Steps, p. 61-62; variant Dealing with Emotions, p. 42-43.

FEAR AND AVERSION

KEE-HUJA'S BAD NIGHT

Some thoughts on aversion.

There was once a Tibetan man called Kee-huja who was travelling alone and at night through a place said to be haunted by evil spirits. He was very tired so he decided to set up his camp and get some sleep. During the night he was woken by a tiny, squeaky voice that seemed to be whispering his name, 'Kee-huja'. At first he wasn't sure if he was imagining it, so he sat up and listened carefully. Again he heard the tiny voice, 'Kee-huja'. He was really frightened. 'This must be the voice of an evil spirit!' he thought.

Then he noticed some horsemen riding through the darkness towards him. Terrified, Kee-huja jumped onto his horse and rode as fast as he could. After a while he decided to stop and listen for the voice. There it was again, still whispering his name, 'Kee-huja'. He looked back and saw that the horsemen were still riding through the darkness towards him, and they were gaining on him. Frantically he started riding again. He rode as hard and as fast as he could. After a while he decided to stop again, but the same thing happened.

This continued for many hours, until, frightened out of his wits, Kee-huja rode all the way back to his home. When he got there he told everyone how he had been chased by ghosts. Once he had calmed down a bit, he decided to go to bed. But when he climbed into his bed he heard the tiny voice again, 'Kee-huja'. And he panicked, 'Oh no! The evil spirit has followed me all the way home!' Then he realised that the voice wasn't a voice at all, it was the sound of him breathing in and out of his nose.

When we react to experiences with a lot of aversion, we will suffer. We cannot run away from fear: fear is the wish to run away from something.

Living without Fear, p. 33-34.

THE ROBBERS OF KHAM

Why we should not panic when danger looms.

In Kham, where I come from, there used to be lots of robbers and highwaymen. The first thing they did before deciding whether or not to rob someone, was to see how easy it was to scare them. If they could scare them, then they robbed them. If they could not scare them, then they decided it was too dangerous and left them alone.

There was a band of robbers who lived on a trade route in a remote area of Kham. One day they saw a man coming along the road. He had a rifle, a pistol, a sword and a good horse. The robbers decided to come out of their hiding place and walk towards him to see if he would be frightened. When the man saw them, he jumped off his horse, ran behind a rock and took out his rifle. Some of the robbers thought he must be a very dangerous person and that they should leave him alone. But then they noticed he had taken out his pistol as well, and they realised that he was scared. So the robbers went after him and robbed him of his rifle, his pistol, his sword, and his horse.

On another occasion, this band of robbers saw a different man riding along the road. He didn't have a rifle, or a pistol, or a sword. The robbers came out of their hiding place and tried to scare him. But he rode straight towards them. When he got to the group one of the robbers stepped forward and asked him if he had any snuff. The man replied, 'Yes, you want some snuff?' The robber told him that he did. So the man pulled out a snuff box, took the robber's hand, and put some snuff into his palm. Then, whilst looking directly into the robber's eyes, he tightened his grip, until it almost made the robber cry. 'Do you want any more?' he asked the robber. Very politely the robber said, 'No, thank you very much'. Then the man rode off and nobody followed him.

If you are scared, people are more likely to attack you because, as with animals, fear brings out their aggression.

Living without Fear, p. 36-38.

XV

ATTACHMENT

THE MONKS AND THE
BEAUTIFUL YOUNG WOMAN

An illustration of the meaning of distraction.

There is a story of two Japanese monks who were travelling together and arrived at a river where they met a beautiful young girl who could not cross the river on her own. So the elder monk took her on his back and carried her across. When they had reached the far bank, he put her down and they went on their way. The younger monk did not say anything. But he felt strongly that the elder monk had not behaved properly.

After some time he asked, 'Do you remember the young woman we met at the river? Was it proper for a monk to carry her across? She was a beautiful lady'.

The elder monk turned to him and said, 'I left her by the bank of the river. Are you still carrying her?'

This shows how we usually become distracted. Distraction has nothing to do with our sense perceptions as such. Our senses are always open. We cannot shut them even if we wanted to. Our pattern of making up things in our mind and creating so many images is the source of all our problems. This is the way the samsaric state of mind is produced. We need to abandon that state, and the only way to get out of it is to go back to the pure and original state of our mind, which is free from contrivance. This is the meditation we try to do.

Daring Steps, p. 201.

EAST, WEST, HOME'S BEST!

Two stories about attachment and letting go.

There was once a Tibetan living in the place I came from. He lived along the river in the worst imaginable place. It is situated in a narrow valley between two mountains and there is no view of anything but the dark cliffs on both sides. The sun never shines there, so it is a very dreary place. This fellow went on a pilgrimage to Lhasa and all over Tibet. When he returned he said, 'I travelled all over the world, and there is no place better than this sweet home!' He was simply accustomed to it.

There is another story that tells how somebody went to hell and was there for a long, long time – he had been really bad! After many, many *kalpas*, he had served his time and was leaving the hell realm. He was going up to the white light or something like that, and he looked down and said to those left behind, 'Please, save my seat, don't let anyone else sit in my place!'

This story demonstrates how we often get attached to negative or painful experiences. It is then hard to let go, because this clinging keeps us stuck, trapping us in situations that are not nice or good.

Dealing with Emotions, p. 41-42; variant *Ngöndro*, p. 37.

THE TAR BABY

Letting go.

If you slap the tar baby, your hand gets stuck in it. If you pretend that it is not there and you want to pass by, you step on it and get stuck in it. Whatever you do, you somehow get stuck in the tar baby.

It is like that with emotions. If you push the emotions away, you get stuck in them. Of course, if you hold on to them you get stuck too!

Dealing with Emotions, p. 47.

A Zen Story

The achievement of non-duality.

A Zen story describes a scene in which a master and student are meditating together. Rain is falling, and its sound disturbs the student. The master tells him, 'Just be one with the rain, then it can't possibly disturb you'.

Our perception of things is constantly confused, because of the various concepts that we attach to them. As a Buddha's mind has no duality, he has no feeling of separateness; hence he has no feeling of aversion or attachment to anything.

Path to Buddhahood, p. 151- 152.

XVI

ACCEPTING ONESELF, TRANSFORMING ONESELF

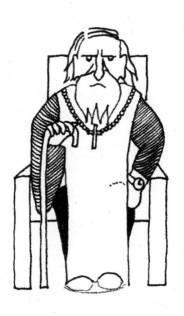

THE PRIEST'S EPITAPH

A teaching on working on ourselves.

It is said that there was once a priest, somewhere in Scotland. He was an old man and just before he passed away, he asked his followers to write an inscription on his tombstone where he was to be buried. In essence it was something like this:

'When I was young I was very enthusiastic and I wanted to change the whole world. So I prayed, "Please, Lord God, give me the wisdom and the power to change the whole world". I tried my best but as I grew older I found that nothing had changed. Then I came to understand that actually I have to change my near and dear ones first, and if they change, the world might change, taking them as an example. I prayed to the Lord God, "Please give me the power and wisdom to change my near and dear ones". And I tried my best again.

When I became very old, however, I found that still nothing had changed. Then I came to know that actually I must change myself first. If I changed myself, maybe some of my near and dear ones would change, taking that as an example. And then, taking them as an example, maybe the world would start to change. Now I pray to the Lord God, "Please give me the strength and wisdom to change myself". But alas, now it is too late.'

Change has to start within oneself, and if you spend all your time trying to change others, you may find it's too late in the end to change yourself.

Dealing with Emotions, p. 11;
variants *Confusion Arises*, p. 193, *Bodhichitta* p. 18-19.

A Child's Expectation of Life-Span

Our expectations of ourselves and others are frequently unrealistic, and lead to negative assessments.

Once, a couple came to me with their child. The child was maybe ten or twelve years old. The parents were very worried. They told me, 'Our child thinks that he will have a short life, that he will not live long. Can you say some prayers? Can you talk to him? We are quite at a loss over it'.

They came and we talked and I asked the child, 'How long do you think you will live?'

The child answered, 'Maybe around seventy years'. The parents were very relieved! The child had the idea that to live for seventy years is a very short life.

Everything is relative. We constantly compare ourselves with others, and this makes us feel we're not good enough or even hate ourselves. If we try to accept the way we are, with all our problems, with all our weaknesses and without looking at the way others are all the time, then nobody needs to hate him or herself.

Dealing with Emotions, p. 3.

THE PATH OF RUDRA

The symbolic meaning of the name 'Rudra'.

The name 'Rudra' goes back to a person who lived a long time ago, long before the Buddha Shakyamuni, and who was the son of an extremely wealthy man. His name was later used symbolically to denote a person who perverts the tantric teachings.

One day, he went to see a very eminent Lama. He was accompanied by a servant, and they both asked for instruction. Having received the same teachings, they went back to study and practise them. Some time later, they came together to discuss the experience and understanding they had gained. To their astonishment, they found that they did not agree on anything. Their viewpoints were diametrically opposed to each other, so they decided to go back to their teacher to find out who was right. Their teacher listened to them both and said that the servant's view was correct. At that, the master was extremely hurt. 'You are no longer my teacher!' he exclaimed. 'You are totally biased and even side with my servant. From now on, I will not listen to you or anybody else. I will do as I think fit! I will follow my own judgement and do whatever I deem right.' With these words, he left and practised his own idea of the teachings.

By doing everything as it should not be done, he gained a very strong negative power. A long time later, he was reborn as a person who was very powerful and at the same time extremely evil. At that time he was called 'Rudra'. He managed to conquer almost the entire world, and spread his negativity wherever he went. Even the gods trembled at his sight, and he held everyone under his sway, including the spirits. No one was able to stand up to him. In this situation, some people turned to his former teacher and servant, who by then had become highly enlightened beings. They asked them for help, saying that they were the only ones with the power to bring an end to Rudra's doings.

In the light of their karmic connection from the past, they got together and confronted Rudra, who was engaged in his usual violence. They transformed into a horse and sow, and then entered his body; once inside, they expanded themselves, causing him unbearable pain. Since they were inside him, Rudra could not do anything against them. From within, they reminded him of his evil deeds. They exhorted him to repent and taught him the right course of action. Then he remembered the former words of his teacher, and this time he understood. Out of heartfelt remorse, he offered his body as an example of someone who, from being very evil, suddenly transforms into the positive. From then on, his outer appearance has been used as a symbol within Vajrayana practice. Once subdued, he himself became a protector of Dharma as a wrathful deity.

Negative actions always have negative results and cause suffering, but there is a way out of this suffering and negativity.

Daring Steps, p. 142-143.

THE GREAT HINDU MASTER WHO COULD WALK ON WATER

What must I change to be free from suffering?

There is a story about a great Hindu master who once lived in Calcutta, and who could walk on water on the River Ganges. Some of the college students went to him and requested him to teach them how to walk on water. They repeatedly asked him so that finally, he said to them, 'See that boat on the river?'

'Yes', they said.

'See how easily it goes on the surface of the water?' he said.

'Yes'.

'I think it is better to get a boat if you want to go on the surface of the water. It is much quicker and much easier than learning how to walk on water!' He told them it was more economical and easier, more beneficial, to learn how to row a boat than to learn how to walk on water. Even if you could learn how to walk on water, it would take so long to learn and then, afterwards, if that is the only thing you can do, it may not be so useful. So maybe it is not the best way, not the best use of your time.

In the same way, we should change some things in life for the better, if we can. But eventually it is our way of reacting we need to work on. This is the way in which there is a real possibility to free ourselves. The problems will not necessarily all go away, but how we look at them and how we react to them – how we experience our problems and our life – will be different.

Journey from Head to Heart, p. 84-85.

XVII

LETTING GO

The Rich Men and the Fisherman

Learning to relax and enjoy what we already have.

Once, two rich men were rushing to go sailing on their beautiful yacht. A fisherman was sitting on the beach with his fishing-rod. The two men stopped in their tracks and approached him. They asked him, 'What are you doing? Why aren't you doing something useful?'

The fisherman responded, 'What do you think I should do?'

They shouted, 'You should work. You are in the way!'

'Well', asked the fisherman, 'what will happen if I work?'

'You will get money', insisted the two.

The fisherman enquired, 'What should I do when I have money?'

The rich men told him, 'Then you can do more work so that you can get more money'.

And the fisherman asked again, 'What should I do when I get more money?'

'Then you will become rich and can invest your money', agreed the two.

'What should I do when I become rich?' asked the fisherman.

The two men beamed, 'Then you can do whatever you like'.

The fisherman nodded, saying, 'Ah, yes, and that is what I am doing right now!'

Both negative and positive emotions can become a habit, a pattern. The more relaxed you are, the less tense you are and the more joyful you become. Happiness is not the destination, or the goal; happiness is the way.

Dealing with Emotions, p. 64-65.

THE ZEN MONK AND THE THIEF

Why we should extend compassion to those who commit negative acts.

Once there was a Zen monk in retreat in an isolated place, and he kept some money in a wooden box. One day when he was not there, someone came, prised open the box, and took the money. When the monk returned and found his money gone, he realised he could not get it back, and so he decided to dedicate it. He said, 'I dedicate this money to whoever took it. May it benefit him greatly and may this dedication turn him into a good person'. With this prayer the incident was over for the monk.

Some time later the police arrested the thief. They brought the money-bag to the monk and asked, 'Isn't this your stolen money?'

The monk said, 'Yes, this is my money, but he did not take it. I freely gave it to him'.

At that the police could do nothing and had to set the man free. The thief was deeply stirred by the monk's noble-mindedness. He came back to the monk and offered him the money-bag, saying, 'Please take this. I never knew that there could be anyone generous enough to forgive someone like me. You must be my guru'. From then on, the thief became a student and totally reformed his way of life.

We may not be able to act like this monk, but at least we should try not to harbour any negative feelings, no matter what happens. Keeping hatred alive is harmful for ourselves as well as for anyone we meet. We should try to let go of whatever we have lost and dedicate it to the one who caused the loss, wishing that it may turn into utmost benefit for that person. In this way our deprivation transforms into generosity.

Daring Steps, p. 85.

XVIII

IMPERMANENCE AND DEATH

MILINDA QUESTIONS NAGASENA ABOUT LIFE AFTER DEATH

The Buddhist concept of rebirth.

Milinda was a Greek king, who ruled in the Kashmir area of India. At that time there was an Indian scholar-saint named Nagasena. The king invited him and asked him many questions, such as, 'How do these changes take place, how does life continue into another life and then become a rebirth?'

Nagasena answered in this way, 'Nothing goes from here to there'. But how could that happen? He went on to say, 'Suppose you light a candle or a butter-lamp, how long will it last? Well, the butter-lamp may last all night, if it is a big one. The flame you had at the beginning, the flame that continues throughout the night, and the flame at the end of the night, is it the same flame or not? It has been burning continuously from the moment the lamp was full, through all the different hours of the night, and then there was only a small part of the lamp left. Could it be one and the same flame? It has been burning continuously throughout the night, so you cannot say that it is just one flame. It is the continuation of a flame. But at the same time you cannot say that it is different, because it is the same flame'.

When we die, there is a state we call bardo, the in-between state. At that time we are not a single mind but a complex aggregate. At this point we do not have a material physical body as we do now, but we have a mental body. For this mental body, one moment continues into another, one moment changes into the next. In this way the whole process never stops. Rebirth is this continuity. What transfers from one life to another is therefore not a single entity. It is both identical to and different from, the previous life.

From Milk to Yoghurt, p. 9.

EXTRACTS FROM STORIES ABOUT THE EARLY KARMAPAS

Explanation of the Tibetan origin of the Tulku.

The recognition of a Tulku, the recognition of a rebirth, is very Tibetan. The concept was also accepted in India, but the recognition of the rebirth of Lamas, from one life to the next, more or less started in Tibet.

Maybe you know this story about the Karmapa? In the 12th century in Tibet, there was one Lama who later came to be called Karmapa. He was told by his teacher that he must build three monasteries, two in Kham and the third one in central Tibet near Lhasa. During his life, Karmapa built the two monasteries in Kham, and when he was around eighty years old he told his students, 'I must go and build the third monastery I promised my guru'. So although he was very old, he travelled to central Tibet. There he built a little hut, but then he died. But before he died, he said, 'Do not dismantle any of the things I have done, and do not give away my books and other things, but keep them. I will come back'.

After a few years a small child appeared and said, 'I am Karmapa'. So everyone said, 'Alright, you are Karmapa!' He was then trained over time by Lamas of different traditions and he turned out to be an extraordinary person. He stayed with the Sakyapa Lamas, who at the time were very famous. Maybe you have heard about the adventures of Marco Polo in Kublai Khan's time where these Tibetan Lamas used to make and stop rain, or make a cup come up to your lips unaided? It was the second Karmapa who was supposed to have done these things.

The Karmapa served as Chogyal Phagpa's ritual master for some time and travelled to Mongolia and China with him. Chogyal Phagpa was the first Tibetan Lama to rule Tibet. Later, the second Karmapa became the teacher of the Mongolian Kings and, by the time of his death, he had become very famous.

The third Karmapa was recognised by a student of the second Karmapa, the student's name was Urgyenpa. He was a highly regarded Lama who went to India many times, a great sage and scholar. When the third Karmapa was still in his mother's womb, Urgyenpa said, 'Your child will be born a boy, and he will be the rebirth of Karmapa'. This was the first time in Tibetan history, maybe in the history of the world, that a certain child was recognised by another person as being the rebirth of a previous person. This child was very special. When he grew up he remembered everything about his past, and not only that, he also remembered all his experiences in his mother's womb. He actually wrote an autobiography about his time in his mother's womb!

The tradition of recognising rebirths began in Tibet. People in Tibet respect these Tulkus, as they are known, and so far they enjoy a good reputation.

From Milk to Yoghurt, p. 10-12.

IMPERMANENCE AND DEATH

THE DYING MAN'S INSTRUCTIONS TO HIS SON

Reflexions on the complexity of human relationships.

There is a story from Kashmir. Once upon a time, there was a father and his son, and before he died the father gave his son a great deal of advice on various matters. However, there were two things which were quite confusing. One was that he should never walk in the sun when he went to or from his shop (he was a shopkeeper), and the second was that he should marry a new wife every day. He had always been an obedient son, very respectful towards his father, so he thought he must do whatever his father had told him and moreover (besides these two confusing points), all the other instructions his father had left were very good. He was facing a big problem.

At last, after having searched for a long time, a beautiful girl accepted the deal. The ceremony was prepared and he asked her once more whether she was sure to agree to marry him, because the next day, he would divorce her and marry someone else. She answered that it was all right. The next morning, when he asked her to go, she refused and told him that he had misunderstood his father's instructions. His father didn't mean that he should marry a new girl each day, but that he should treat his wife every day as if they had just married that day. He thought she was probably right, that this might be true, and they lived together very well for a long time.

Then, because his father had told him not to walk in the sun, he was just sitting inside and not going to work and his business was declining. His wife told him that he had misunderstood yet again, and what his father really meant was that he should go to his shop before sunrise and come home only after sunset!

If we really understood impermanence we would treat our wife or husband as if we were newly-weds and give them all our love, because our time together can end at any time.

Ngöndro, p. 25-26.

HAPPINESS IS ELUSIVE

The transience of life.

It was the custom in the monasteries of Tibet for each elderly monk to be responsible for the training of younger monks and they would all practise Dharma together. One old monk gave his students a great deal of studying to do. In return, he promised to take them on a picnic as a special treat, if they worked hard at their learning. But each day, when they had finished one exercise, he gave them another and the picnic never took place. They were always too busy. One day the teacher and his students were out walking through the countryside and they saw a group of people in the distance. The old monk had very poor eyesight and he asked, 'Who are those people? What are they doing?'

One of the brightest students answered him, 'Oh Master, someone has finished all his work and now they are taking him on a picnic as a special treat!' However, when the monk and his students drew closer to the group, they discovered that it was not a picnic but a funeral procession and the people were carrying a body to its burial.

We can spend our whole lifetime preparing for happiness. We wait for the time when we can really enjoy ourselves but the moment never comes. Time runs out. At death, all of our hopes and activities come to an end and only then do we truly find any relief from our busy schedule.

Mind Training, p. 5-6.

The Couple Who Lost a Son

A Jataka story on impermanence.

There was a family consisting of an older couple, their grown-up son and his wife, and their grandchild. The family lived closely together, and they loved and respected each other so much that they became an example to their whole village. Everyone thought that they were a model family. One day the grown-up son died. The neighbours were shocked and said among themselves, 'This is terrible! His old parents and wife must be devastated'.

The neighbours went to console the family, and when they arrived they found, to their astonishment, that the rest of the family was acting as if nothing had happened. Neither his parents nor his wife were in mourning, everything seemed quite normal. No one could believe their eyes and they asked the father, 'What is this? Your son died, didn't he?' 'Yes, my son died', the father said. His neighbour asked, 'How is it possible that you are not sad and mourning for him? We thought that you had a wonderful family who loved each other dearly, but we must have been wrong'.

The father said, 'We were very affectionate and never said or did anything hurtful to each other, because we always knew that our being together would not last. We knew that each of us could die at any moment and we would be separated. With the understanding that we had only a short time together, we were able to be close and kind to each other. My son has gone, but I knew that this might happen any time, so it is not a shock. Of course, I am not happy. But during the time we lived together, we did whatever we could to help each other. Now, my son has died, but I have no regrets. I am thankful to have had this opportunity'.

IMPERMANENCE AND DEATH

Of course, it was the Buddha himself who made this statement in one of his former lives, and it is not so easy to develop this attitude. But when we know in our hearts that by having come together we will naturally be separated sooner or later, there is neither reason nor need to fight. We should use the opportunity of being together as best we can. If we truly understand impermanence, we will be able to relate to people more wisely.

Daring Steps, p. 74-75; variant *Path to Buddhahood*, p. 35.

DEDICATION

All my babbling,
In the name of Dharma
Has been set down faithfully
By my dear students of pure vision.

I pray that at least a fraction of the wisdom
Of those enlightened teachers
Who tirelessly trained me
Shines through this mass of incoherence.

May the sincere efforts of all those
Who have worked tirelessly
Result in spreading the true meaning of Dharma
To all who are inspired to know.

May this help dispel the darkness of ignorance
In the minds of all living beings
And lead them to complete realisation
Free from all fear.

Ringu Tulku

USING STORIES AS TEACHINGS

The following is the edited transcript of an interview, which Ringu Tulku graciously accorded me during a month-long retreat at the Bodhicharya Meditation Centre in Sikkim in November 2012.

Editor - Rinpoche, you very kindly agreed to talk about your use of stories in your teachings. I would like to start by asking you where you get these stories from; do they have different origins? What memories do you have of being on the receiving end of stories, of hearing stories in your childhood, your youth?

Ringu Tulku Rinpoche - Firstly, I love stories; I'm crazy about stories. I remember when I was only about three years old, I was already running after people who were telling stories. I remember my great-aunt, who died when she was around ninety or something like that – she was a student of Jamgön Kongtrul the Great – she used to tell stories, and I would listen to them and beg her to tell them again and again and again, because it seemed to me that she was there doing nothing but reciting her prayers! And then there was another lady who worked for us, milking the cows, making cheese, making the yak dung into dried cakes, making tsampa, that sort of thing; she used to be good at storytelling, and I used to follow her wherever she went. I didn't allow her a moment of peace while she was trying to work and do things: I was beside her all the time, and sometimes mother used to tell me off!

Then I had my old aunt, Ani Palo, who died here [in Gangtok], actually, at the age of ninety-three. She was a good story-teller; I always used to be with her, asking her to tell stories and so forth. Her husband, a very kind, nice gentleman, also knew lots of stories. He used to make toys for me as well. He had very good hands, so he used to make toys, carved out of wood, all sorts of things, and then he'd create stories from the toys he made. I had a big box of toys that he'd carved for me.

Ed. - The toys would come alive...?

RTR - Kind of... That sort of thing. But this situation relates to traditional life in Tibet; we had no television, no radio, so in the evenings people told stories instead. We would lie down, sometimes in the tents, but a lot of the time outside, because that's where we would sleep, looking up at the stars. And then people would tell stories. So story-telling used to be a very common thing in those days. Actually, the Dharamsala Tibetan Library asked me to write a series of Tibetan folk-tales, and I started the project. But I wrote only one book of the series; I couldn't do the rest. It was published in Tibetan and later in Hindi and German. Some other people translated it into English and published it without my name!

I feel that I learned a lot about life through these folk-tales. I think people can learn about life, about death, about relationships, about all aspects of life, from stories. To me it's very important, very interesting. Children especially, I think, should hear stories, in their original form, not edited. Nowadays stories have become too watered-down, too edited, too 'safe'; they've taken all the life and death out of them...

Ed. - They've become 'politically correct'...

RTR - Yes, they've become much too 'politically correct', and so children don't know anything about life. I'm very annoyed when people say 'Babies are brought by the stork'. What does that mean? Or 'It's Father Christmas who brings all the sweets and things'. Why should you tell lies to your children? It means that very quickly, you no longer have any trust in your parents. I think that's a very bad start. It seems to me that it's very important to know life as it is. It makes you mature, it makes you see the world much more clearly.

Ed. - Are some of these stories getting completely lost? I'm thinking particularly from the children's perspective. Are children still hearing them from their parents, their grand-parents?

RTR - That's the problem. I think it happens less and less. Nowadays, in my family, for example, I don't think anyone is telling stories any more. They're just watching the TV. The parents themselves probably don't know many stories either, and even if they do, they know only the ones they read in books. Maybe in the rural areas of Tibet, stories are still being told. But I think that wherever a more modern way of life has been introduced, storytelling is in decline.

So that's how I first got interested in stories. Then of course, when I learned how to read, in Tibetan and English and Hindi and other languages, every time I get a story-book I just can't put it down. I have to I finish it.

Ed. - You're saying that in the present tense: so you still do that?

RTR - Maybe a little less now, because I have too many other things to do. But yes, I do, although nowadays I retain a little less. When I was young, whenever I heard a story, I never forgot it. But now, I often forget it. That's the difference that age makes!

I myself used to tell stories from a young age. I would tell stories to my brothers and sisters, folk tales, things like that. But sometimes just stories that I made up. I used to entertain them in this way for hours and hours and hours. I could go on telling them stories all day.

Ed. - And these were sometimes stories that you invented?

RTR - Many of them I invented. And sometimes they were very, very long stories...

Ed. - Much better than the television for keeping them quiet, anyway.

RTR - But then I read whatever stories I can lay my hands on.

You were asking me earlier about the Gesar stories. These bards are a different phenomenon. It's a different thing, very special, a kind of paranormal phenomenon. The story just comes to them, and then they can tell it for days and days and days without stopping. They're not memorizing anything; the words just come to them. And they can tell exactly the same story many times. It's something quite extraordinary. The Chinese have also got very interested in this. They have got a big Ling Institute in Peking. I have heard that the longest recitation they have recorded runs to 165 volumes. It's a very big thing altogether, but different.

It was also a tradition to read the Gesar stories. You would sing, and you would read the actions. The way that the Gesar stories are written is that all the actions are in prose, and the dialogues are in verse, so you sing the dialogues, for which there exist many different tunes. I used to take part in these readings. Actually, when we were first in Sikkim, in the evening, there would often be Gesar reading and recitation and many people would gather for it. There was one old lady in particular, who was very interested. She would ask me to read, so every evening she would light a kerosene lamp, and then make some soup. I'd go along, with lots of other people, and I'd read. Sometimes other people would join us, in an impromptu way, as the night went on. That's more or less how I learned to read.

Ed. - And that would be singing, chanting, would it, or just reading?

RTR - Singing and chanting.

Ed. - Because it's in verse...?

RTR - All the dialogues are in verse, the real story is in prose. So you read the story in prose, then when you come to a dialogue you sing. You can sing alone, or you can sing with two people, or three people...

Ed. - Because of course the fact that the dialogues are in verse helps the bard to memorise...

RTR - No, it's not memorised, it's never memorised. It's impossible to memorise it, there are volumes and volumes of it. We read it again and again, and that's the way we used to do it.

Then, on top of that, when I was seventeen, I was appointed as the Tibetan text-book writer. My job was to write text-books in the Tibetan language for the schools of Sikkim and to train Tibetan teachers to teach them. We had a big children's library, and that was my office.

Ed. - What a wonderful job for someone like you!

RTR - Yes, a wonderful job! I really enjoyed it. It was the best part of my life. Just reading stories and children's books for eight whole years. Also at that time there was a king and a queen, and the king also used to collect folk-tales in Sikkim, and I would accompany him. He had a tape-recorder, and we used to go from place to place to record; we'd find out who had some stories, and we'd go there and ask that person to tell those stories and we'd record them. Later on we'd transcribe them.

He would also sometimes organise story-telling sessions. On behalf of the government of Sikkim, we would invite elders from the villages of Sikkim, and the king and queen would be there. And then the king used to serve them *chang* – you know, this local millet beer – and then they'd tell stories. They felt obliged to produce their stories, since the king and queen were there. We did that quite a few times. So I had a very nice job. And that's why I know a lot of stories.

Ed. - When you went round collecting stories, were they mainly being told by old people, or people of all ages?

RTR - All sorts of people. Generally we think that old people will have more stories, but I find that that is not necessarily the case. It varies from person to person. Some people remember, maybe they just have more interest in these things. Some people maybe heard the stories, but they just don't stick in their minds. As for me, I used to retain the stories I heard, but now I've forgotten everything like that!

So going around the villages in this way, we got quite a few stories. It was not always easy, and some people were critical, but because of my interest, and because I got so much from them, I persisted.

There are lots of other stories in the Tibetan Buddhist tradition, Jataka stories, for example, that the Buddha himself used to tell, and that are teachings about everything in Buddhism.

And there is also a special kind of book, called a *pejö*, that's a teaching through maxims and stories. I taught a little bit of that in Samye Ling once. This teaching is called a *Kadampa pejö*, and through the stories and proverbs that it contains, the whole of Buddhism is taught, from the concept of the precious human life to all the six paths.

Ed. - And are these collected, or are they created especially for the teachings?

RTR - They're collections used for teachings.

So as you can see, my stories are from everywhere: Tibetan sources, Indian sources, any story I can find. Sanskrit is also very rich in stories, and when I was studying Sanskrit, I also got into lots of story-books. There's the *Pancha Tantra* and the *Hitopadesh* and things like that. Actually, the *Pancha Tantra* is very interesting. The story is as follows: once upon a time there was a king, and this king had five sons, princes, who were very spoilt by their father, the king. So when he wanted to educate them, nobody could do the job, because they were so utterly spoilt. They didn't want to study. Then the king got rather frustrated, and announced that if there was anybody who could educate them they would be given a very big reward.

After some time, a rishi responded to the king's appeal. You know that at that time in India there were those hermits called rishis, who lived in the forest, and sometimes had students, though they didn't create regular schools. So this rishi came to the king, and said: 'I can educate your children, but on one condition: that I take them away to my ashram'. The king agreed, so the rishi took them to his ashram in the forest. He told them a story every day, and after six or seven months, he brought them back, and said to the king, 'They're educated now'. And that was the case: they were educated, just from hearing daily the stories in the *Pancha Tantras,* the 'five tantras'. It seems that if you read and understand these five tantras, you're educated! This tradition is still maintained; I used to read them myself.

Anyway, there are lots of stories of this kind. And on many occasions, when I'm teaching Dharma, these stories come up to illustrate some point, because I'm familiar with them.

Ed. - What is it that conditions whether you use stories or not? It's fairly clear that in some teachings there are a lot of stories, and in others there are not very many, or hardly any at all.

RTR - Sometimes it's because of time. When I'm teaching a text, and I'm trying to go through it, explaining and commenting on it, making points, and it has to be finished within a certain number of days, if you then tell a lot of stories, you'd never finish it. I could be teaching the same book for ten years. Sometimes though it's because of my mood, the stories just don't come.

Ed. - Does it depend on the audience at all?

RTR - Of course it might depend on the audience too. Also on the circumstances: when it's more leisurely, and you have a little bit of time, when it's in the countryside, and it's relaxed and people don't have to rush off, the stories tend to come. And then sometimes I tell stories if people seem to be a little bit dull, or about to go to sleep, or the teaching is getting a little bit too serious, or it's in the middle of the day, and it's hot: in that kind of situation, I try to bring in a story or something like that to wake them up!

Ed. - Because there's a theatrical element to teaching, after all.

RTR - Yes: sometimes when you're going through some very serious material, after some time people can't take any more, because it's too heavy. Then you need a break to bring them back. I'm not the only one using these methods; I know of several teachers using stories as a resource. There's an Australian Theravadin monk, Ajahn Brahm, for example, who has written a very beautiful book of stories entitled *Opening the Door of your Heart*, and another with the title *Who Ordered This Truckload of Dung? Inspiring Stories for Welcoming Life's Difficulties*. He's using these stories in his teachings. I met him last year, when I was in Indonesia for a conference.

Then there are also collections of stories under the general title *Chicken Soup for the Soul*; there are now 200 titles, the first compiled by Jack Canfield and Mark Victor Hansen.

I also once met an American Dzogchen teacher, Surya Das, who published a collection of stories with Daniel Goleman under the title *The Snow Lion's Turquoise Mane: Wisdom Tales from Tibet*. We planned to write some books together, but somehow it didn't happen. There are other very good books of stories, in English, written by Buddhist teachers.

So there's no shortage of modern collections of stories, and of other teachers using this kind of material. And then, going back to the tradition, in the *Dhammapada*, for example, each stanza is illustrated by a story. The *Vinaya*, too, is full of stories; each precept has a story accompanying it, some of them very interesting. So, you see, stories have been part of the Buddhist tradition from the earliest times up to the present day. And I'm very happy to help in keeping that tradition alive.

Sources Used

Bodhichitta, edited by Cait Collins, Lazy Lama Series, No. 4, Bodhicharya Publications, 2001; 2nd edition, 2014

Buddhist Meditation, edited by Cait Collins, Lazy Lama Series, No. 1, Bodhicharya Publications, 1998; 2nd edition, 2013

Chenrezig: The Practice of Compassion, transcribed and edited by Corinne Segers with further editing by Caitlin Collins, Rigul Trust, 2011

Confusion Arises as Wisdom: Gampopa's Heart Advice on the Path of Mahamudra, commentary by Ringu Tulku, translated by Ringu Tulku and Ann Helm, edited by Ann Helm, Shambhala, 2012

Daring Steps towards Fearlessness: The Three Vehicles of Buddhism, edited and translated by Rosemarie Fuchs, Snow Lion Publications, 2005; reprinted as *Daring Steps: Traversing the Path of the Buddha*, Snow Lion Publications, 2010

Dealing with Emotions: Scattering the Clouds, edited by Mary Heneghan and Marion Knight, Heart Wisdom Series, Bodhicharya Publications, 2012

'Rebirth: A Buddhist View', in *From Milk to Yoghurt: A Recipe for Living and Dying*, Transcribed by Maria Huendorf, edited by Marita Faaberg, Margaret Ford, Ringu Tulku and the Bodhicharya Publishing team, Heart Wisdom Series, Bodhicharya Publications, 2009

Journey from Head to Heart: Along a Buddhist Path, edited by Mary Heneghan, Heart Wisdom Series, Bodhicharya Publications, 2012

Like Dreams & Clouds: Emptiness & Interdependence, Mahamudra & Dzogchen, Heart Wisdom Series, Bodhicharya Publications, 2011: *Emptiness & Interdependence*, transcribed and edited by Mary Heneghan and Jonathan Clewley; *Mahamudra & Dzogchen*, transcribed and first editing by Corinne Segers, second editing by Margaret Ford and Patricia Little

Living without Fear and Anger, first transcribed by Brigit Habetz, edited by Andy Powers, Lazy Lama Series, No. 5, Bodhicharya Publications, 2005; 2nd edition, 2013

Mind Training: Lojong, the Seven Points of Mind-Training, transcribed and edited by B. M. Shaughnessy, DHI Publications, 1995; 2nd edition substantially revised, 2003

The Ngöndro: Preliminary Practices to Mahamudra, transcribed and edited by Corinne Segers, 1996; further editing by Maggy Jones, 1997-98 and by Ringu Tulku, Margaret Ford and Tim Barrow, 2008, Heart Wisdom Series, Bodhicharya Publications, 2008

Path to Buddhahood: Teachings on Gampopa's Jewel Ornament of Liberation, edited by Briona Nic Dhiarmada, Maggy Jones and Corinne Segers, Shambhala, 2003

Refuge, Lazy Lama Series, No. 3, Bodhicharya Publications, 2000; 2nd edition, 2014

Please note: in the interests of accessibility, and with the exception of *Mind Training*, I have used the 2nd edition of texts referred to, where one exists.

ACKNOWLEDGEMENTS

I gratefully acknowledge the following contributions:

NiL Éditions (Éditions Robert Laffont) Paris, for permission to use extracts from *Path to Buddhahood*, DHI Publications, London, for extracts from *Mind Training: the Lojong of Ringu Tulku* and Rigul Trust Publications for extracts from *Chenrezig - the Practice of Compassion*. Shambhala Publications for extracts from *Confusion Arises With Wisdom: Gampopa's Heart Advice on the Path of Mahamudra* and *Daring Steps Towards Fearlessness: The Three Vehicles of Buddhism*.

Kagyu Samye Ling for the Chenrezig thangka painted by Sherab Palden Beru, reproduced by kind permission of Victoria Long. Photograph by Peter Budd.

Mary Heneghan in her editing role, for her close attention to the text, her advice based on a long-standing knowledge of Ringu Tulku Rinpoche's teachings, and her encouragement throughout.

Rachel Moffitt and other members of the Bodhicharya Publishing team for their enthusiasm and encouragement from the early stages of the project. And to Rachel Moffitt for help with proof-reading.

Annie Dibble for suggestions arising from an attentive reading of the final version.

Ani Wangmo for advice on Tibetan terms and spellings.

Margaret Richardson for the text of 'The Start of the Bodhisattva Path'.

Conrad Harvey for the spirited drawings that embellish the text.

Paul O'Connor for his expert and elegant work in designing the final product.

The regular army of transcribers and editors of the stories in their oral form, whose work in many cases remains anonymous, but who otherwise are acknowledged in the 'Sources used' section, and without whom this anthology could not have been produced.

Friends and fellow Dharma-practitioners, whose support in times of doubt proved invaluable, in particular Pat Murphy who, in an illuminating email exchange on reading the final text, showed me what I was doing, and restored my faith in it.

All my teachers, both formal and informal, who prepared me, consciously or unconsciously, to undertake this project.

My husband Roger, whose expertise in the mysterious ways of the computer helped me out of many a hole, and who proof-read the manuscript in its latter stages.

And most of all, Ringu Tulku Rinpoche, for his open-hearted belief in the project, for graciously allowing me to interview him on the use of stories in his teachings, and for all those story-rich teachings so generously offered over the years to his students all over the world, upon which this work is entirely based.

Such inadequacies and defects that remain in the finished text are my responsibility, and mine alone.

Patricia Little

ABOUT THE AUTHOR

Ringu Tulku Rinpoche is a Tibetan Buddhist Master of the Kagyu Order. He was trained in all schools of Tibetan Buddhism under many great masters including HH the 16th Gyalwang Karmapa and HH Dilgo Khyentse Rinpoche. He took his formal education at Namgyal Institute of Tibetology, Sikkim and Sampurnananda Sanskrit University, Varanasi, India. He served as Tibetan Textbook Writer and Professor of Tibetan Studies in Sikkim for 25 years.

Since 1990, he has been travelling and teaching Buddhism and meditation in Europe, America, Canada, Australia and Asia. He participates in various interfaith and 'Science and Buddhism' dialogues and is the author of several books on Buddhist topics. These include *Path to Buddhahood, Daring Steps, The Ri-me Philosophy of Jamgön Kongtrul the Great, Confusion Arises as Wisdom, the Lazy Lama Series* and *the Heart Wisdom Series*, as well as several children's books, available in Tibetan and European languages.

He founded the organisations Bodhicharya - see bodhicharya.org and Rigul Trust - see rigultrust.org.

OTHER BOOKS BY RINGU TULKU

PUBLISHED BY BODHICHARYA PUBLICATIONS:

The Heart Wisdom Series:

- *The Ngöndro:*
  Foundation Practices of Mahamudra
- *From Milk to Yoghurt:*
  A Recipe for Living and Dying
- *Like Dreams and Clouds:*
  Emptiness and Interdependence,
  Mahamudra and Dzogchen
- *Dealing with Emotions:*
  Scattering the Clouds
- *Journey from Head to Heart*
  Along a Buddhist Path
- *Riding Stormy Waves:*
  Victory over the Maras

The Lazy Lama Series:

- *Buddhist Meditation*
- *The Four Noble Truths*
- *Refuge:* Finding a Purpose and a Path
- *Bodhichitta:*
  Awakening Compassion and Wisdom
- *Living without Fear and Anger*
- *Relaxing in Natural Awareness*

PUBLISHED BY SHAMBHALA:

- *Path to Buddhahood:* Teachings on Gampopa's 'Jewel Ornament of Liberation'
- *Daring Steps:* Traversing the Path of the Buddha
- *Mind Training*
- *The Ri-Me Philosophy of Jamgön Kongtrul the Great:*
  A Study of the Buddhist Lineages of Tibet
- *Confusion Arises as Wisdom:*
  Gampopa's Heart Advice on the Path of Mahamudra

ALSO AVAILABLE FROM RIGUL TRUST:

- *Chenrezig:* The Practice of Compassion - A Commentary
- *The Boy who had a Dream:* An illustrated book for children

For an up to date list of books by Ringu Tulku,
please see the Books section at

www.bodhicharya.org

*All proceeds received by Bodhicharya Publications from the sale of this book
go direct to humanitarian and educational projects because the work involved
in producing this book has been given free of charge.*

INDEX OF STORIES